Inner
Excellence

Inner Excellence

Achieve Extraordinary Business Success Through Mental Toughness

JIM MURPHY

New York Chicago San Francisco Lisbon London Madrid Mexico City
Milan New Delhi San Juan Seoul Singapore Sydney Toronto

The McGraw·Hill Companies

Library of Congress Cataloging-in-Publication Data

Murphy, Jim, 1967–
    Inner excellence : achieve extraordinary business success through mental
toughness / Jim Murphy.
        p.   cm.
    ISBN 978-0-07-163504-2
    1. Success.   2. Success in business—Psychological aspects.   I. Title.

BF637.S8M79   2010
650.1—dc22   2009037851

2 3 4 5 6 7 8 9 10 11 12 13 14 15 16 17 18 19 20 21   DOC/DOC   5 4 3 2

ISBN   978-0-07-163504-2
MHID   0-07-163504-1

Interior design by Susan H. Hartman

McGraw-Hill books are available at special quantity discounts to use as premiums and
sales promotions or for use in corporate training programs. To contact a representative,
please e-mail us at bulksales@mcgraw-hill.com.

Finally, brothers, whatever is true, whatever is noble, whatever is right, whatever is pure, whatever is lovely, whatever is admirable—if anything is excellent or praiseworthy—think about such things.

—Philippians 4:8

**For
Naomi T. Murphy**

**My sister,
my inspiration**

Contents

Foreword.. ix

Preface: Presuppositions............................ xi

Acknowledgments.................................... xv

Introduction...................................... xvii

1 Maslow and the Maserati 1
The Pursuit of More

2 The Monster of Self 25
The Biggest Obstacle We All Face

3 The Quest for Fearlessness 51
Three Pillars of Extraordinary Success

4 Code of the Samurai 73
The Triumph of Mastery over Ego

5 Change Your State, Change Your Life 93
How to Get the Feelings You Want

6 The World Is Flat 113
Reconstruct Your Model of the World

7 **A Clear and Present Beauty** 135
The Four Most Powerful Ways to Be Fully Present

8 **Poise Under Pressure** 159
Four Keys to Extraordinary Performance

9 **Zoë and the Mind-Set for Growth** 181
The Underlying Process of High Performance

10 **Maslow, Michael Jordan, and the Navy Seals** 203
Three Hallmarks of Extraordinary Leaders

Conclusion: A New Way of Life 221
Notes 227
Glossary 241
Index 247

Foreword

For more than thirty-five years I've pursued a career in excellence. This subject has intrigued and challenged me both as a professional athlete and as a coach to hundreds of thousands of individuals and hundreds of the best corporations in the world.

Today more than ever, excellence is an elusive quest for most of us. Information has never come to us with such swiftness and abundance. Our thoughts are overloaded from cell phones, texting, CNN, FOX News, Facebook, YouTube, Twitter, and other social media. Chaos is increasing while excellence and, ultimately, productivity are decreasing. The average Fortune 500 CEO, for example, receives more than 175 e-mails on a daily basis. Wow! That's overload. This increase in thought has stolen our simplicity and life balance. It also threatens our ability to achieve the extraordinary while living a fulfilling life.

Extraordinary performance and a balanced life, for my clients and seminar attendees, has been my life's work. Occasionally in my career, I come across rare individuals who not only think differently but also live and teach others how to do the same. Jim Murphy is one of those individuals. His clients have achieved tremendous success, and that is no accident.

As soon as we met, I immediately recognized his passion for excellence and the art form of achieving it. After spending a lot of time with Jim, I understood that he lives his writings and his talk. He is inquisitive, determined, intelligent, and open-minded. His ideas on what holds us back are profound. Jim has captured the essence of excellence in a manner that's both engaging and powerful.

We all face adversity and have fears that constrain us. Jim shows us how to use that energy to be totally engaged in the moment. His approach to surmounting the obstacles in our highest pursuits not only is simple and clear but also is backed by compelling stories of people who have achieved the extraordinary.

Jim's success in turning teams around has been phenomenal, and *Inner Excellence* shows you how you can do the same with your life, career, and entire organization. Managers and employees will learn the powerful techniques Jim has taught to Olympic and professional athletes, such as how to lead with your heart, expand your vision, and perform with passion in the most pressure-filled moments.

As you read this book, you will learn to overcome your fears and embark on a journey of great personal and professional achievement. You'll gain a clear understanding of the pathway needed to find true inner peace and happiness.

Jim Fannin, "Change Your Life" Coach
**Author, *S.C.O.R.E. for Life: The Five Keys
to Optimum Achievement***

Preface
Presuppositions

This book was written for those who want to live fully and achieve greatly. If you'd like to be better at what you do and live a more fulfilling life, you're in the right place. In order to do that we must consider possibilities, find new ways of thinking. For starters, we can model the thought patterns of remarkable people who live passionately and achieve extraordinarily. Below are examples of some of those thoughts, called presuppositions. A presupposition is a useful belief that helps achieve desired outcomes.

- Every thought and image in your mind has a consequence.
- The mind and body are intimately connected; each affects the other.

- Development of the whole person (mind, body, and spirit) is the most powerful way to create the best employee, manager, teacher, or athlete.
- We live simultaneously in two worlds: the tangible world we can see, touch, taste, etc., and the unseen world that controls the tangible world. When we learn how these unseen forces shape our lives, we can consistently change our lives and those of others for the better.
- There is no failure, only feedback. The outcome of your actions becomes a failure the moment you label it as one. Your judgment determines that label.
- The unconscious mind runs our lives, constantly working to maintain homeostasis—attracting circumstances and people compatible to what we unconsciously believe. These beliefs can be changed.
- Underlying every behavior is a positive need or intention. Human behavior is not random. There is a purpose behind every behavior, and it is always done in some way to try and fill a need for something positive.
- People make the best choices available to them. Any behavior, no matter how strange or screwed up, was the best choice available to him or her at that moment in time (given that person's life history, knowledge, beliefs, and resources, and viewed from his or her frame of reference).
- We all have a naturally biased, self-focused frame of reference from which we view the world.
- Our self-focused frame of reference leads to self-consciousness, one of the biggest challenges we face.
- You cannot *not communicate*. Everything you do or don't do sends a message.

- The meaning of your communication is how the receiver takes it. No matter how well-intentioned your communication is, how ever the receiver understood or took your communication is the meaning.
- The person with the most behavioral flexibility has the greatest ability to influence others and achieve his or her goals.

As you go through the book, keep these presuppositions in mind, especially in the first two chapters as we analyze the challenging obstacles that we all encounter. As you do, you'll begin to notice how some of these perspectives will help you gain mastery over your greatest challenges. This will set the foundation for the tools and skills you'll learn throughout the rest of the book.

Note: Whether these presuppositions are always true is irrelevant; the important thing is that they are beliefs held by extraordinarily successful people, and modeling them will help you achieve your goals and dreams. Many of these presuppositions are similar to or derive from those of Richard Bandler and John Grinder, the founders of neuro-linguistic programming (NLP).

Acknowledgments

I've been so blessed to have an amazing team of people around me. Natasha McCartney, my Vancouver-based editor, has been truly incredible and giving with her time, energy, and talent. My agent, Rita Rosenkranz, has held my hand every step of the way from the proposal to the final product. Ron Martirano, my editor at McGraw-Hill, has been a huge help.

Special thanks to Olympian Heather Brand, who has contributed so much to this project. Her insights, feedback, and support were an incredible gift.

Thanks to my early readers and great friends John Kehoe, Jennifer Seo, Ricky Scruggs, Nick Osborne, Peter Little, Richard Lopez, Mark Kinsey, Robert Ratajczyk, and Romeo Bolibol. Thanks to Harry Nichols, Darrel Johnson, Blaine Croy, Toshimi

Watanabe, Shawn Mulligan, Nina Durfee, and David Dressler. Thanks to Ken Shigematsu, whose teachings and friendship have taught and inspired me. Thanks to David Chao and the gang at Lean Sensei International.

I'd also like to thank the following:

Dr. Jack Curtis, of the Seattle Mariners; Ronn Svettich, of the Colorado Rockies; Mike Grouse, of the Texas Rangers; Jim Fannin, and Tom Trebelhorn, Major League Baseball manager and coach, for the many conversations we've had on high performance.

Dr. Cal Botterill, Dr. David Coppel, Dr. Ken Ravizza, Dr. Doug Newburg, Dr. Jim Bauman, Dr. Jim Loehr, Dr. Matt Brown, and the many other sport psychologists who have contributed their thoughts and wisdom.

The Navy Seals I met with and all the business leaders, athletes, and coaches—many of my own clients—who've been so helpful.

The University of British Columbia men's golf team, for their inspiration and dedication in pursuit of a courageous life.

Lewis Gordon Pugh, for inspiring all of us to find a purpose beyond ourselves.

My parents, who also read the manuscript and gave their thoughts, as well as love and guidance my entire life. My brothers, Dave, Pat, and Mike, and my sisters-in-law, Arlene and Betty, who have all supported me in many ways these past five years working on this project. My sister, Naomi, the incredible inspiration. Most of all, thanks to God, who has blessed me greatly.

Introduction

The real test of courage is not to die, but to truly live.

—Conte Vittorio Alfieri

Life is filled with choices. Where you go, what you do, and who you become are the result of daily decisions you make. There is one decision that outweighs all the rest, and that is: will you be true to yourself in a world trying to make you like everyone else? What does that even mean? You may be endlessly pursuing goals to have more, win more, achieve more—all of which could be wiped out in one economic tidal wave. Is the path you're on taking you where you really want to go? When you're on your deathbed looking back on your life, will you have peace and fulfillment with no regrets?

In my experience talking to and working with world-class performers and leaders, I've learned that what we really want, beyond our tangible goals and pursuits, is fullness of life. We want to have great experiences and use our full potential. We want to be challenged, we want to be creative, and we want to grow. We want freedom to live with passion and pursue our dreams regardless of what people think, how much money we make, or level of status we acquire. Ultimately, we want to vividly experience great moments in our life and live fully.

Fear takes all of that away. Instead of challenges, fear sees obstacles; instead of opportunities, setbacks. Instead of experiencing growth, we live in the past. If we want to truly live, we need to embrace our fears and find the courage to be our true selves.

As an outfielder in the Chicago Cubs organization, my self-image and self-acceptance revolved around my batting average. When I hit well, I walked tall and felt great. When I hit poorly, my shoulders slumped and my outlook was dark. Life was a roller coaster of emotions. I was a slave to the results, and it stifled my performance.

When I started my coaching career, I saw this over and over again: athletes had lost the joy of performing, and their passion for life, as they struggled under the pressure to win. The fear of failure engulfed their lives.

In my research on fearlessness, I came upon British adventurer Lewis Gordon Pugh. In 2007 he took a Russian icebreaker to the arctic circle to swim one kilometer in below-freezing ice water. He wore only a Speedo, cap, and goggles. You'll read about how, though filled with fear and contemplating the real possibility of death, he made a powerful difference on an international scale. You'll also learn how others around the world have used his same strategy, and how you can too—because it works.

This book is about extraordinary performance and long-term fulfillment, at the office, on the field, and at home. We'll look at world-class performers who live balanced, fulfilling lives and study the key principles that allow them to do that. We'll look at the unique life perspective of extraordinary people, including how they've learned to direct and control their feelings and compete to win without becoming enslaved by their performance.

We'll see how the basic principles are the same, whether you're an athlete or an executive, an Olympic team or a small business. We'll explore the concepts of self-actualization and the ways in which the study of extraordinary people teaches us to perform our best and truly live.

This is a book based on a presupposition: the biggest obstacle we face, in performance and in life, is self-centeredness. It's not the morality of it that I speak of. The main issue is that in our preoccupation with ourselves, our vision narrows, our growth is limited, and our failures are amplified. You may not think you're self-centered, but consider this: is not everything you think, say, and do based on your experiences, your goals, and your beliefs? How you see the world, and therefore what you believe is possible, derives from you—or more precisely, who you perceive you are. That perception comes from your mind's continual assessment of your past, to which you become attached. It's that attachment that limits us. Our biggest obstacle is in our mind, or, rather, the program our mind runs based on who we were.

The solution is one that has empowered world-class performers, Olympic and professional athletes, and some of the best businesses in North America. It's a model based on three simple words: love, wisdom, and courage. Love is to lead with the heart, wisdom is to expand your vision, and courage is to be fully present. In this model, love becomes passion, wisdom becomes purpose, and courage becomes poise.

Any athlete or executive, as well as any team or organization, can achieve extraordinary success with these fundamentals. If in the pursuit of the extraordinary you focus on love, wisdom, and courage, you'll find, I believe, that extraordinary experiences, not winning or the bottom line, is the key to extraordinary performance.

Maslow and
the Maserati

The Pursuit of More

Seduced by the siren song of a consumerist, quick-fix society, we sometimes choose a course of action that brings only the illusion of accomplishment, the shadow of satisfaction.

—George Leonard, aikido master

Freedom is costly. In order to be truly free, we must conform to a certain discipline, face our fears, and connect with our true selves. The path toward real success and long-term fulfillment is a risky one. Obstacles of materialism, consumerism, and instant gratification confront us every day. They create a seductive numbness that inhibits a powerful life. As we gradually conform to the world and its definition of success, we become enslaved to our performance, lose our freedom and, eventually, our selves.

It's a scary view, the risky path of our true dreams. We get comfortable in the easier route of less risk, less failure, and more self-indulgence. We don't like to look at that thorny path of possibility; it's not comfortable. It's easier to give in to that part of the mind that wants instant gratification and temporary pleasures, to cover up the bigger, scarier picture of what we really want: the sacred moments that come from feeling truly alive. So we end up chasing success, or chasing numbers, or things, or money as a substitute for the deep need to feel grounded and fulfilled, using our God-given talents.

We've all had times when everything seems to flow—sacred moments, when we're caught up in the action in the midst of performance. When we do glimpse those sacred moments, for a split second at least, we wish we had the courage to pursue this path with all our heart. And we can. It's just that often we're so hard on ourselves, amplifying all our failures and regrets, that we neglect to see what's still possible—a life centered and connected, one that empowers others.

The aim of this book is to help you capture those moments. We'll look at how top Olympians and world-class performers train for years for an event that may last less than a minute. We'll see how they are able to stay in the moment and perform their best, under incredible pressure. Then we'll establish how you can do the same, whether you're an athlete or an executive, regardless of your sport or profession.

It makes sense if you think about it. We all want essentially the same things: we want great experiences and to be part of something. We want to love and laugh and be successful. It's human nature. But each of us also has a mind that entertains negative thoughts, produces desires that hurt us, and creates beliefs that limit us. This all occurs in a mind that's never been trained to manage the one component on which everything hinges: our thoughts.

In the pursuit of extraordinary performance it's easy to succumb to anxiety and pressure, because so much is out of your control. When you learn to be fully engaged in the moment, however, then you can perform your best *and* love the competition. Every performance, presentation, or business meeting is an opportunity to learn, grow, and vividly experience each moment. You will find, as you take this journey with me, that extraordinary performance is a subset of extraordinary experience.

The Narrow Road to Self-Actualization

In the quest for a courageous life, there are two basic paths: the popular road, spacious and inviting, searching for things that bring praise and admiration; and the one that, though difficult, less glamorous, and often rocky, leads to confidence, inner peace, and fulfillment. It's the latter path that sacrifices much but holds the key to extraordinary performance. There you'll find freedom, focus, and confidence and not be attached to what people say.

This is the path that interested psychiatrist Abraham Maslow. He analyzed the characteristics of extraordinary people—how they thought, what they dreamed of, the way they lived. In doing so, he found that they shared a number of common traits, including a strong sense of self, a close connection to others, and both the curiosity to solve problems and the creativity to do it. They had high self-acceptance and were motivated to have peak experiences. He called these people who not only changed the world but also lived fulfilling lives *self-actualizers*. Self-actualizers, he noted, shared a unique ability to engage in moments in which they felt truly alive, creative, and integrated. Maslow described eight elements of self-actualization:

1. **Total absorption.** This element represents the ability to experience key events fully, vividly, and selflessly, with complete concentration.

2. **Growth choices.** Life is a process of choices, one after another, between safety (out of fear and the need for defense) and risk (for the sake of progress and growth).

3. **Self-awareness.** Your thoughts and actions should be in tune with your authentic self instead of merely conforming to your culture. Self-awareness allows you to understand and identify the distinction.

4. **Honesty.** When practiced by self-actualizers, honesty goes beyond telling truths to others and means looking within yourself and taking responsibility for your actions.

5. **Intuition.** You cannot count on making wise decisions unless you dare to listen to your intuition. As a self-actualizing trait, intuition is as much about having instincts as it is about having the courage to follow them.

6. **Self-development.** Making real one's potential is a never-ending process. For each of us to move forward, we must

always be in a state of development and avoid "resting on our laurels."

7. **Peak experiences.** The conditions for these transient moments of self-actualization can be set up so that they are more likely to occur.

8. **Lack of ego defenses.** Maslow felt that we build walls to protect ourselves but that instead they hem us in. We must first identify our internal defenses and then find the courage to give them up.

For Maslow, these elements and the behaviors associated with them reveal what's already within you, or—more accurately, as he says—what is already you. Imagine Michelangelo chiseling away the marble block as he sculpted David. He cut away everything that wasn't David to expose this magnificent human form. We are the rock with the potential to emerge into something incredible, but we're constrained by expectations, worries, and fears. We've been socialized to value the fame and popularity of success, however fleeting, over the experience that drives it. In this we lose our joy. We get so locked into winning that we become afraid of losing.

Attachment to something of which you're not in complete control makes you needy and brings with it the fear of not getting what you really want. Back and forth it goes, between the focus on winning and fear of losing. Tension rises as the pressure mounts. But beneath those constraints that bind lies the heart of a warrior—the true you. Remove what is not you, and as with Michelangelo, you'll unveil tremendous strength and poise.

The Affluenza Virus

To chisel away what's not you is difficult. It is easy to get sidetracked, seduced by the facade of what looks like your true dream. Our North American culture injects us daily with an externally oriented focus—what some refer to as the "affluenza" virus. This virus craves four things: money, possessions, achievements, and status. Its viral effect plants the constant desire to gain more and compare yourself with others—and it never gets satisfied. This phenomenon distances you from your true self.

In my observations of other cultures, life appears simpler. In Costa Rica, for example, lawyers, cabdrivers, and tow truck drivers all seemed equal socially. A lawyer may socialize with a tow truck driver (and invite the person in for dinner after having his car towed, as my host family did while I was there coaching). The Costa Rican culture seemed far happier than my own. They worked. They ate. They played. They lived. In their developing country, they needed little and appreciated much.

Ironically, in North American culture, it's our fixation on the symbols of our dreams that takes us further from the dream inside us. A nicer car. A bigger house. A more prestigious anything. Our natural attraction to things that make us feel and look good is where the road diverts from that which is powerful, fulfilling, and permanent.

According to Maslow, when we spend our lives pursuing nicer places to live and faster cars to drive (even if they are really cool), we're being sidetracked by low-level needs. The problem is not the components of the virus in and of themselves—the money, achievements, and so forth—but rather putting your trust and identity in something transient and unstable. The real problem occurs when those external things become your ultimate treasure, because your heart will follow. The focus of your highest desires molds you into that which you desire. Money, possessions, achievements, and status are all fleeting, and a heart built on temporary things will have insecurity as a constant companion.

As others praise or covet your possessions or achievements, you get a momentary sense of pride and false sense of worth, which spurs you to get more of what you were praised for. The cycle spirals and becomes a sickness that leads to despair as you unknowingly become identified by what you have or what you've done. It leaves an emptiness. Søren Kierkegaard, in his book *The Sickness unto Death*, said most people have a sickness they carry until they die; it's a despair that many don't even know they have. The affluenza virus is similar, quietly replacing passion and fulfillment with temporary satisfaction. If you really want a great life, don't get sidetracked by cultural facades.

Pursuing Ghosts

In the thoughtful book *Season of Life*, Jeffrey Marx chronicles the unique coaching style of former NFL star Joe Ehrmann, now a volunteer assistant at Gilman High School, in Maryland. Ehrmann's career in the NFL seemed outwardly successful, but it left him feeling empty. He explains:

> I had expectations that professional football would help
> me find some kind of purpose and meaning in my life. But
> really, all I found in the NFL was more confusion. I kept
> having the belief that if it wasn't going to be this contract, I

would certainly find some kind of serenity or peace in my life with the next contract, the next girl, the next house, the next car, the next award, when I got to the Pro Bowl, when we got to the Super Bowl. And what happened to me I think happens to an awful lot of professional athletes: you start losing perspective. You've kind of climbed the ladder of success, and when you get up there, you realize somehow the ladder was leaning on the wrong building.

Joe realized that he had been socialized to pursue ghosts of what he really wanted. "The single biggest failure of society [is] we simply don't do a good enough job teaching boys how to be men," he says. In his desire to be a man, he pursued a false masculinity by trying to validate himself as he grew up through his athletic ability, sexual conquests, and economic success. "Masculinity, first and foremost, ought to be defined in terms of relationships," Joe asserts. "Success comes in terms of relationships. The second criterion—the only other criterion for masculinity—is that all of us ought to have some kind of cause, some kind of purpose in our lives that's bigger than our own individual hopes, dreams, wants, and desires. At the end of our life we ought to be able to look back over it from our deathbed and know that somehow the world was a better place because we lived, we loved, we were other-centered, other-focused."

Joe's uncommon approach comes from firsthand experience in pursuit of the American dream, a dream that didn't deliver on its end of the bargain. What Joe wanted was something more real than trophies, more meaningful than money. As he played pro football, he found that the external symbols of success brought instant gratification and were alluring, but they diverted his attention away from the qualities that would carry him throughout his life.

The trap Joe fell into, and the virus that afflicted him, is one that gets to most of us. We all want to be successful, but what does that mean? Often people say that they just want to be happy, but even that concept is difficult. We're not very good at knowing what makes us happy. We want real and true happiness, peace, and fulfillment, yet every day, we are presented with potential shortcuts that undermine this pursuit. There's always a promotion, a raise, or all-star status on the horizon that steals the limelight and dulls the senses toward the process in the middle. Things such as love and sacrifice get pushed aside. (Note: in our discussion, love is not sexual. It's passion for life, connection with others—a powerful, positive energy.)

It's natural to want to skip the in-between. When our goal to get to the next level in our career is powered by the affluenza virus, we do not find meaning in the process; all that matters is the bottom line, win or lose, the end result. We wind up losing sight of the reason we want the things that we do, which is the feelings they give us. We live for feelings and experiences, and most of what we do is based on them.

Do you have the virus? One of the symptoms is the sense of entitlement that comes to those who are infected. When you've grown used to a certain amount of "worldly success" and your identity has become intertwined with it, you'll feel a deep disturbance when someone or something threatens to take away from you that for which you've worked so hard. It's become a part of you.

Perhaps the most influential part of the virus is not the lust for more, but rather the lust for more than anyone else. The "more than you" issue is the fire under the simmering viral brew.

In later chapters we'll discuss how we get in our own way and succumb to the insecurity of the affluenza virus. We'll also look at how "self-actualizers" overcome the obstacles we all face in our quest for inner excellence and a fearless life. To better understand the challenges before us, we'll first take a closer look at how our culture molds us, specifically through the various media and the vast influence they have on our lives.

The Fuel for the Virus

In this age of technology and consumerism, we're inundated every day with media messages urging us to get more, have more, and achieve more. We're constantly pushed to take that first path and judge ourselves by how we compare with everyone else. The powerful audio and video components of television and the Internet (TVI, for future reference) seep into our subconscious and program our minds with each viewing. Big business marketers know this very well, of course, spending millions of dollars for thirty-second opportunities to focus our thoughts and influence our desires.

TVI stifles your ability to think creatively, uniquely, and for any length of time on one thing, or on *no* thing. "Television watching, one of the signature activities of our culture, correlates with brain problems," says Norman Doige, M.D., author of *The Brain That Changes Itself*. Television, with its short-attention-span technology and the convenience of being able to rewind scenes, trains us to pay less and less attention. The Internet's endless sea of words teaches us to skim rather than read. Pro baseball manager Tom Trebelhorn says, "We're in a replay society. I don't have to pay close attention, because I can replay it. Our social environment doesn't lend itself to preplaying [visualizing the next task], which inhibits imagination." We're cultivating ourselves to be attention deficient—or, you could say, addicted to instant response.

TVI scatters our energy with its focus on materialism, consumerism, and instant gratification, sidetracking us from the reasons we want the things it promotes, which are the feelings we hope they'll give us. What we really want is a high quality of life (HQL)—measured by such traits as passion, peace, fulfillment, and peak experiences.

The constant media connection between materialism and success generates a strong association with HQL. The mind, with its propensity for pattern recognition, triggers the unconscious day after day to associate these symbols with the feelings of HQL, however misleading. That trigger soon gets rusty, though. Pretty soon the feelings go click instead of bang, until one day there's no click at all. The feelings that were once so strong and vibrant soon fade, succumbing to the anesthesia of worldly success and admiration. We become numb as we continue to try to excite those feelings with more and more temporary external things, when inside we are searching for something more permanent and fulfilling.

In this society, the affluenza virus is everywhere and everybody seems to be afflicted. When everyone around you has the cold or flu, it's hard not to get it yourself; you must take measures to strengthen your immunity against it, or you will succumb as well. Your immunity, as you'll see as we go along, is strengthened by attributes such as a strong sense of self, a purpose that transcends cultural influences, and a powerful system for managing your thoughts, feelings, and desires.

Sport psychologist Dr. Keith Henschen says that living in a society that is externally motivated is one of the two biggest obstacles to peak performance (the other being overanalysis). Without our knowing it, the world spinning under our feet lures us into a constant desire for things that we can't fully control, that come and go, that we can never have enough of.

The Obsession with Winning

In a society structured around instant gratification, it's a challenge to be true to yourself and transcend enculturation the way Maslow's self-actualizers did. To be true to yourself is to do the following:

- Seek self-awareness and develop your intuition.
- Realize your unique value.
- Know how you want to live, so you can feel energized and fulfilled and compete with freedom.
- Connect with and empower others.
- Have a meaningful purpose and a vision that serve this purpose.

One of the major struggles many people have is getting caught up in the outcome, to the detriment of focusing and performing. Winning is, after all, "the American way." It's the storybook ending: hitting the home run in the bottom of the ninth, scoring the winning goal, or getting the big promotion. But winning is temporary and can be cruelly misleading.

Winning has a deceptive attraction because in the media it is strongly associated with peak experiences. However, the fact that you won does not mean you were great, or at your best, or even good. Winning, you could say, is part of both the solution and the problem—it straddles the line between what you really want and the flu-inspired illusion of what you want. Playing to win is an important part of competition, but when winning supersedes living with passion, then it invites tension, doubt, and fear.

The obsession with winning distracts from the process. The goal has become more important than the reason for the goal. In this win-at-all-costs society, you can get your values mixed up, even to the point where athletes are willing to die in five years if they could take a pill guaranteeing a gold medal. The chance for prestige, wealth, and fame is so alluring that people will die to get it. Consider the incredible scandals of corporate greed. Enron, AIG, Fannie Mae, Bernie Madoff—the list goes on. Why do corporate executives risk their careers, lie to their friends and family, and end up in disgrace? They've been seduced, infected by the virus. It's not what they envisioned, of course. It's what happens when who you are and how you affect others get overshadowed by how you compare with others. It's a slow seduction. Ask yourself, does external gratification encompass all you really desire? If you were offered the same chance to get *your* gold medal, would it cross your mind to take the pill?

We've been socialized to sacrifice integrity for winning. That's extremely costly. The price of anything, as Henry David Thoreau said, is the amount of life you exchange for it. To trade our soul for one victory is to get caught up in society's obsession with what's fast and hot and exciting: the 440 horsepower, the Italian mystique, the paddle gearshifts, the wow factor. With no awards (or press coverage) for the discipline, self-control, and hard work that it takes to succeed, the process gets undermined.

Winning the gold medal (or Maserati) is not great because of the medal itself. The greatness lies in the growth, tears, and sweat that went into its achievement. The process of learning to believe in yourself and become more fully you, through all the adversity, is what makes it great.

The best teachers and coaches impart skills such as discipline, courage, and love. They value learning and growth far more than the task they're teaching or game they're trying to win. Legendary North Carolina basketball coach Dean Smith relates, "Our North Carolina players seldom heard me or my assistants talk about winning. Winning would be the by-product of the process. There could be no shortcuts. Making winning the ultimate goal usually isn't good teaching." He adds that former University of Nebraska football coach Tom Osborne believed that focusing on winning could be an obstacle as much as a motivator. Smith points out, "So many things happened in games that were beyond our control: the talent and experience of the teams, bad calls by officials, injuries, bad luck." Defining your success based on factors out of your control undermines the process that got you there, and Smith made sure his players knew that.

The True Price of Win-at-All-Costs

The win-at-any-cost mentality fuels the affluenza virus and invites the pressure and anxiety that impede progress. It threatens to displace who you are for what you (think you) want. Alison W. swam for the U.S. Olympic team at the 1996 Olympic Games in Atlanta. She won a silver medal, yet as she stood on the podium, her only feeling was relief that it was over. She soon developed an eating disorder and quit swimming before her senior year in college. "I haven't been happy in the pool since I was eight years old," she said. In Alison's pursuit of Olympic glory, she lost a lot.

Alison's journey is similar to that of thousands of other athletes: on the outside all seems well, but on the inside they're losing themselves amid all the hype. It's not a true victory when you win outwardly but lose inwardly. As with art and education, sports and business can help you grow and experience life in tremendous ways, but if your goal is to win at any cost, it will truly cost—sometimes everything.

Business executives perhaps have it worse in this regard, because athletes are trained to eat well, rest, recover, and prepare for competition. In the business world so many of us "train" eight to ten hours a day, eat a poor lunch, and then go home and work some more. Rest, recovery, and proper nutrition are easily overlooked, and burnout becomes a real issue.

In North America we've become lazy from a culture of affluence, one structured around instant gratification. Our obsession to win has literally taken us to the moon, but it's also created a culture that wants things right away, fears failure, and readily forgets the sacrifice and teamwork involved in doing great things. Habits start to form in which we take shortcuts, pills, and payoffs in order to "succeed." Life soon becomes a Pavlovian experience in which the bell is rung and we salivate for instant success, to feel good now. Author Joseph Campbell says, "We've become nothing more than a predictable pattern of wires responding to stimuli." In our "flu"-filled culture, it takes more and more to be happy. (Unlike the Costa Ricans, who live and love regardless of economic position.)

If we want to achieve big goals, we must suppress the impulse for instant gratification. To have restraint is to not be ruled by feelings and emotions and the easier, forget-our-problems solution. Discipline is the ability to focus our desires on what matters most, and as psychologist Jim Loehr says, make our sense of honor greater than our moods. We all have desires, but it's where and how we focus that desire that will determine our success.

Fast-Forward to the Future

I worked with an athlete recently, Andrew B., who was not only talented but obsessed with winning. As the captain of one of the top collegiate volleyball teams in the country, he made his sport his life. His energy and will to win were rarely matched. The downside was that Andrew's obsession with winning at times overshadowed his love for playing. He and his team struggled. Then things changed.

Andrew visualized his legacy by fast-forwarding his life to his eighties. He thought of the things he hoped to leave behind and recognized that they were not centered around winning volleyball games. He also realized that his present-day identity came from his sport and that it fluctuated by how well he played and how many games his team won. Andrew started keeping a journal and questioned what he really wanted in life. He realized he wanted to learn and grow and have great experiences, and he wanted to use volleyball to help him do that, and not be enslaved by his performance. In his quest of self-discovery he learned how to be true to himself and his teammates. His last two seasons were the team's best in more than two decades. Now playing professionally in Europe, Andrew remembers, "I was so caught up in volleyball and winning that I lost sight of the process and how it all fits in the big picture."

In a culture of constant comparison with others, it's easy to lose sight of who you really are—your true self. Your true self is defined not by what you have, what you do, or what others think of you, but rather by how you use your gifts to empower others. The greatness within you cannot be defined by a role or responsibility or label, however grand or meritorious.

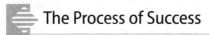 The Process of Success

To be true to yourself is to focus on winning the toughest battle, the one within. This battle is a daily journey filled with moments that have more meaning and are more rewarding than the final score. International bestselling author John Kehoe (*Mind Power into the Twenty-First Century*) tells a story about a trip through Tibet, where he witnessed a sandpainting project in progress. In a local market, maroon-robed monks worked diligently, day after day, creating the intricate forms that made up the mandala. Different colors of sand were used, and each detail was completed with the utmost attention. There were six or more monks working on it at any given time. Each day when he returned to the market, John looked forward to seeing what new designs had been created. It took more than a week to finally finish the painting. An elaborate ceremony followed, and then something totally unexpected happened: all at once they destroyed the painting. The hundreds of man-hours that it took to create this beautiful masterpiece were wiped away in a single moment. John said, "I was stunned. This action defies our Western sensibilities. Our Western notion of labor is that we work in order to achieve a result. It is what we produce from our effort that is important. But to the Buddhist *it is the process that matters, not the final achievement. It is the attentiveness to each moment.*"

The importance of focusing on process over outcome struck me when I was coaching at the 2000 Sydney Olympics. I had attended the women's 4 × 100 track-and-field relay race and was heading back to the Athlete's Village. I got on the bus and noticed the gold medal–winning team there with me, along with a few other athletes and coaches. To my astonishment, instead of displaying high fives and jubilation, the newly crowned champions simply stared straight ahead in silence. There were many possibilities to explain the hushed bus—fatigue, relief, and so forth—but what stuck with me was that the gold medals around their necks were external objects that didn't necessarily impact their internal world, let alone bring happiness.

Winning and losing are so similar, yet their effects on us are vastly different. Consider a race where one athlete has a personal best time yet loses by a tenth of a second and the winning athlete does not match his personal best. Who ran the better race? For most of us, the emotional ties to the outcome of our performance are so strong that they obstruct our vision and focus. We are so attached to winning that we become afraid of losing, which takes away the freedom and joy. When we can "meet with Triumph and Disaster and treat those two imposters just the same," as Rudyard Kipling said, then we won't feel betrayed as much by the false sense of security that winning can bring, nor will we miss all the good in a loss. Colorado Rockies performance coach Ronn Svetich explains, "Success and failure are exactly the same. Once you understand that they're allies and not enemies, now you can make friends with failure, by quickly learning from it. When you play the student role during failed outcomes, then your trust doesn't go down, because you've learned what to do next time, and now you feel better about yourself."

What we really want in life is not to win a game or a medal; what we want is to live with passion, to have great experiences, to learn, grow, and be challenged. Losing is an emotional letdown to most of us, but what we learn and experience along the way is crucial feedback for a better tomorrow.

Winning is not the best measure of success, because you can't control it or sustain it—not how you'd like to, anyway. Also, you may win, but it may not be your best performance, or even a good one. Three-time national champion basketball coach Mike Krzyzewski describes his approach:

> If we're constantly looking at our win-loss record to determine whether we are doing well, we're not looking at the right barometer. If you're always striving to achieve a success that is defined by someone else, I think you'll always be frustrated. There will never be enough championships, never enough wins. And when you finally attain them, if you're lucky enough to do so, they'll only be numbers. Somebody will say you were great or successful, but ultimately you'll know it's an empty success. The only way to get around such an unhappy ending is to continually define your own success. Your definition of success should have more depth than the equivalent of winning a national championship. It should be whatever passion moves you deep in your heart.

In the end, the biggest victory is not getting something shiny, fast, and lavish, winning a gold medal, a corner office, or a national championship, but rather winning the battle with yourself. In every performance we undertake, we choose between our attachment to winning and our deep desire for peak experiences, to grow and learn and become more at peace, more stable, and more able to repeat powerful, fulfilling moments. Of course, this frees us up to perform with passion and focus—and to win more often.

To win the internal battle, Jim Loehr says to ask yourself three questions when your day is done: Did I give 100 percent? Did I stay predominantly positive? Did I take responsibility for my actions? Focusing on these questions allows you to win more often and create a path that is not only powerful but also sustainable.

Olympic gold medalist Clara Hughes's clear perspective on why she competes allows her to perform with poise and confidence as a cyclist and a speed skater. Here's part of a journal entry (from Dr. Cal Botterill's book *Perspective*) after one of her Olympic victories:

> For years I have challenged myself in sport. In my heart it is clear to me why I go to the line time and again. I can assure you it's not a medal hanging around my neck that I'm after. Medals are things I send to my Mom in Winnipeg, which she in turn shares with friends and family. They are not what provide the deep sense of accomplishment, which fills my sense of self, in turn teaching me how to live.

When you become obsessed with winning, the increasing pressure brings overanalysis and perfectionism, throttling your focus and enjoyment. Sport psychologist Jerry Lynch emphasizes this point: "When you let go of the obsessive need to win, you decrease your tension, stress, and anxiety and increase your probability of winning." As you find a process that works for you, your perspective will change, and you'll be able to be more fully engaged in each moment. You'll have greater opportunities for peak experiences, regardless of who wins, which, ironically, will help you win.

A Life of Peak Experiences

The reason we want to win or succeed is that we think it will enhance our lives in some manner; somehow it will make us feel good, or it will give us the resources (money, status, possessions) so we can feel good in the future. Our goal of success is really the goal to have great moments in our lives in which we live with passion, fully experiencing all that life has to offer. What the self-actualizers did was look for a way of living by which they could have peak experiences more often. Peak experiences are sacred moments, those times in life when everything comes together, when your mind, body, and soul are unified and challenged in a way that makes time seem to stand still, when the world is perfect in that instant.

Peak experiences start with the heart. To lead with the heart is to live and compete congruently, true to your values. It's the guiding principle for sport psychologist Dr. Cal Botterill, author of the book *Perspective*. He explains: "Somehow top performers have a perspective that allows them to stay *want to*. They don't get into this *have to* and put all this pressure on themselves that hurts their performance. I think this happens a lot, and that's why I've always done foundational psychology, like: Who are you? What are you about? Where's your support? How do you want to live and compete?"

In the pursuit of a courageous life, we must continually learn about ourselves—who we really are and what's truly meaningful. There is only one way to truly know freedom, and that is to find that part of ourself that longs for it and to find exactly what it longs for, beyond the temporary pleasures and possessions that possess us. We must be determined to be disciplined in the right areas, sacrificing pride and status for growth and experience. In this pursuit we can find a freedom that knows no boundaries, one not enslaved by success but instead focused on purpose and others. As we'll see, the natural tendency of the mind can be, well, monstrous in this regard.

In the chapters to come, we'll see how fear stops us and what the root cause of fear really is. Then we'll look at how the world's best performers overcome fear with the powerful virtues of love, wisdom, and courage.

Key Points for Chapter 1

- Living in an externally motivated society undermines the process of high performance.
- The media's hypnotizing effects drive a constant desire for more—one that never ends.
- It's easy to get sidetracked by the symbols of success and become enslaved by our livelihood.
- Extraordinary success is a by-product of performing with freedom and passion, bringing your true self to work each day.
- The pursuit of extraordinary experience allows the process of extraordinary performance to unfold most powerfully.

Follow-Up Questions and Activities

- Examine your life. What gives you your identity? If you find your identity through what you do or what you have, does that give you real peace and fulfillment? If those things or achievements were taken from you, who would you be?

- Imagine you are eighty years old, looking back on your life. What will the one thing be that was most important to you? If you continue to live your life the way you are now, will that be your legacy?
- When you've performed your best in a meeting, a presentation, or an athletic event, what characteristics describe how you were feeling and what you were thinking?
- How does freedom fit into your work and your life? What does it take to feel that freedom?

The Monster of Self
The Biggest Obstacle We All Face

We Western people are apt to think our great problems are external, environmental. We are not skilled in the inner life, where the real roots of our problems lie. The outer distractions of our interests reflect an inner lack of integration of our own lives. We are trying to be several selves at once, without all our selves being organized by a single, mastering life within us.

—Thomas R. Kelly, *A Testament of Devotion*

For most people, it starts out when you are a kid, probably sometime in grade school. You attempt to do something you love—perhaps you're skilled at kickball or you play a mean recorder—and one day something changes. Maybe you're a basketball player about to shoot a free throw with the game on the line, and previously, you would have been completely focused and nailed it. But this time you think, "I've gotta make this." That little switch in perspective is the beginning of a life-long battle. You go from enjoying the moment to *having to* succeed, your heart on one side and your mind on the other.

Your heart, with its dreams and loves and passion, and your mind, with its logic and doubts and fears, are often at odds—but when they unite, it's liberating. When you play from the heart, your efforts are worthy for their own sake; the performance is its own reward. There are no thoughts that interfere, or if there are any, they are crystal clear, efficient and productive. Playing from the heart gives you the freedom to fail, with no worries of the past or future regarding what may or may not happen. It's how you once were until your mind began to get in the way. Your mind has a way of heckling and deceiving you, or just convincing you of your limits. It's a duel between love and logic that never ends.

In our consumer-oriented society, thousands of claims on our attention come at us every day: television, radio, the Internet, e-mail, text messages, Twitter—they bombard us from the moment we wake until the minute we sleep. We have more technology, more time-savers, and less time. In this continuous barrage taking our thoughts in endless directions, we're constantly preoccupied. This zaps our energy and distances us from our goals, and from ourselves, in the process. Our thoughts become the obstacle.

What we do with our thoughts affects every aspect of our lives, determining whether we're focused or scattered, successful or unsuc-cessful, fulfilled or frustrated. Every performance we'll ever have will largely be shaped by this battle in the mind. We've spent most of our lives with the mind doing what it wants, when it wants, and how it wants to do it—not unlike a spoiled child. The control center has gotten out of control. We're attached to our minds and thus can't see the mind for what it is: an instrument that needs to be handled properly, adjusted as needed, and turned off when necessary. In our attachment we get too close to the story. We need to step back and take a broader look.

In this chapter we'll take on the biggest obstacle you will ever face: yourself. We'll review how the mind locks onto the past and projects it to the future. We'll see how it stifles our freedom and struggles to see beyond our failures and past limitations.

The Root Cause of Fear

In my experience and through researching top sport psychologists and world-class performers, I've found that fear stifles our freedom and hurts our performance more than anything else. Fear of failure, fear of rejection, fear of the future. Fear, however, is only the symptom of a more complex issue. The root cause of fear, as I'll explain throughout this chapter, is self-centeredness.

Self-centeredness is not about a lack of niceness, or even about selfishness—it's not a moral issue. The simple reality is that a preoccupation with oneself limits our options and stunts our growth. This may not be the traditional definition of self-centeredness, but it captures the concept that everything we experience is filtered through a lens that is attached to our past. This provides a setting where fear can thrive.

Fear is an inward-focused feeling. "What's going to happen to me?" it asks. Fear comes from looking at our past and then projecting ourselves into the future and not knowing how it will turn out. Our focus on ourselves and our past failures fuels the fear.

Let's say you're about to give a presentation and you become extremely nervous and afraid. What thoughts are going through your head? Perhaps you're thinking, "Will they like what I have to say?" "What if I look foolish?" "Am I good enough to be telling them what to do?" All those thoughts are focused on yourself. It's only natural, of course.

For your entire life you've seen the world from only your eyes. You haven't seen what I've seen or what anyone else has seen—not from the same perspective, anyway. Moreover, your perspective is skewed based on your perception of what you've seen and experienced. Every experience you've had has been within the framework of how it affects *you*. This fact is not good or bad, just limiting. It's through this biased, limited filter that we see the world, and this filter is dotted with memories of past failures.

> In our everyday life, our thinking is 99 percent self-centered.
>
> —Zen master
> Shunryu Suzuki

In our continual preoccupation with ourselves, we cannot help but think about our past. After all, who are we to our own minds but a collection of memories? The unconscious mind remembers every failure we've ever had, and so our preoccupation with ourselves brings with it constant awareness of all our weaknesses, failures, and limitations. For every circumstance you confront, it scans the memory banks for failures in situations similar to the one you're facing now.

Imagine facing a situation in which you've failed in the past. Your mind will remind you of that failure, and this intrusive, negative thought affects how you perform. Your repeated experiences in this situation have created not only memories but also a belief about your abilities. Your mind "learns" from past experiences, depending on how you perceived what happened to you. Thus, instead of your present situation's being a fresh opportunity to perform, it's largely affected by your mind's attachment to history.

In your attachment to the past and our previous failures, you can become self-conscious, concerned about yourself and what others think of you. Self-consciousness is an easy road to go down when you have a list of failures at hand and see them regularly. If you're shooting a free throw under pressure, for example, the task is difficult not just because of the consequences of missing but also because of the thought that you would be the one who missed it. And you've certainly missed free throws before.

Self-consciousness causes concern about who we are and what forms our identity. So, we compare ourselves with others, which is the fuel for the ego. The ego gets its identity directly from the four tangible factors of worldly success linked to the affluenza virus: money, possessions, achievements, and status. Achievements are a predominant aspect of the ego because they're so personal. They allow you to say, "I did this," or "I did that." In our comparisons with others, we gauge what we have and what they have, what we've done and what they've done. Inevitably, there is someone who has more or better possessions or accomplishments, so we want more, because our identity is at stake. The affluenza virus grips us.

The problem is not the quest for achieving; in fact, this book is about achieving the extraordinary. The problem is placing your security in things you cannot control. It's just like with winning: the problem is not winning per se—every champion plays to win;

the problem arises when the end result overshadows the process and you lose yourself along the way.

When our identity comes from our tangible goals, we become attached to them. Since we can't completely control our goals, we become needy. Consequently, we lose our freedom. Attached to our goals, we get attached to our circumstances in order to monitor if we're getting closer to or further from our goals—and our circumstances are what we use to measure the distance we've traveled.

As we become attached to our circumstances, we also become attached to our thoughts. In other words, doubtful thoughts have more power to influence us when we're attached to our circumstances and need certain things to happen. (We'll discuss managing your thoughts in Chapter 5.) Frustration and anxiety emerge when what we feel has to happen doesn't happen. The gap widens between how we want to feel and what we are feeling. The doubts move from external (I won't *achieve my goal*) to internal (*I'm* not able) to personal (I'm a *failure*). Unchecked, our dreams get frozen in fear.

Along this process, three components of the mind fuel the sickness that causes our despair. As part of my work with athletes and other professionals, I've labeled each of these components based on their specific effects: the Monkey Mind, with its endless stream of mostly negative thoughts; the Trickster, with its quiet, deceiving voice reminding you of past failures and projecting them to the future; and the Critic, the part of us judging every circumstance and reacting emotionally to it.

The mind becomes a monster of sorts, as the Monkey Mind, Trickster, and Critic seductively scatter our energy and hold us back from what we dream of doing or becoming.

The Inner Battle

The monster of self is a devious one that at first presents itself as not overly substantial, but, like a crouching tiger appearing small in the grass, it waits to pounce on us in our difficult moments. The strength of the monster is that it seems so insignificant that we don't take it seriously, and as a result, it grows. We are so influenced by the Monkey Mind, Trickster, and Critic that we accept them as natural, and this is their power.

The monster is sly. We're naturally self-centered, and if we don't recognize this predisposition, our self-centeredness will become self-consciousness and can easily culminate in fear. Because we have been self-centered our whole lives, we don't even notice the fallout from our self-preoccupation. It's an easy thing to overlook, and when we get careless, the dominoes fall quickly. One day we're performing well, going about our business focused and confident, and then suddenly everything's off. We start making mistakes and get frustrated. The doubts come, and we make more mistakes. As this continues, anxiety appears as our perspective narrows, and we're consumed

> This is not a matter of virtue. It's a matter of my choosing to do the work of somehow altering or getting free of my natural, hardwired default setting, which is to be deeply and literally self-centered and to see and interpret everything through this lens of self. People who can adjust their natural default setting this way are often described as being "well-adjusted," which I suggest to you is not an accidental term.
>
> —**David Foster Wallace, professor, author**

Figure 2.1 **The Path to Fear**

with the need for some success. The anxiety turns into self-rejection as we personalize our failures and unwanted circumstances. Fear takes over. Figure 2.1 shows how it looks on paper.

Every day we wake up with a decision to make. We can recognize our inherent self-centeredness and take steps away from it and toward the highest quality of life (a journey on which the rest of the book will guide you), or move toward insecurity, doubt, and fear. We have the freedom of choice, and with it comes the capacity for

courage or fear. Because we all have greatness within us, recognizing our natural self-centeredness is in itself empowering. We'll see in the chapters to come the amazing moments that await those who choose to broaden their vision.

The Obsession with Self

Our self-centeredness shows up early. As newborns we learn that our cries get rewarded with food and attention. We learn to orient everything around how it affects us. This survival method stays with us for the rest of our lives, taken as inherent. It's "hardwired into our boards at birth," as professor David Foster Wallace put it. According to Wallace, "Everything in my own immediate experience supports my deep belief that I am the absolute center of the universe; the realest, most vivid and important person in existence. We rarely think about this sort of natural, basic self-centeredness because it's so socially repulsive. But it's pretty much the same for all of us."

When everything is continually viewed from the same angle, through the same lens, and from the same vantage point, there gets to be a level of comfort and acceptance toward it. It's the human experience. We start to have certain patterns of seeing the world, and everything that comes into our viewfinder gets fit into this model, adjusted to all the assumptions, facts, and data we've compiled. But perception is not reality. The map is not the terrain. The challenge of seeing beyond ourselves is so imposing mostly because we don't even notice that this narrow vision is our normal way of viewing the world. We've grown so used to our limited, skewed perceptions that we take them as reality.

One of the issues that arise from being self-centered is the exclusion of others and the world around you. To be self-absorbed is to limit yourself to your own five senses and the knowledge derived from your personal experiences instead of opening up to the unlimited world of possibilities available to you. This narrow focus excludes the ideas, opportunities, and connections that are possible with broader foresight. When your vision is limited by your own needs and wants, your main pursuit can become self-serving, where life moves from growing and improving to self-preserving; hoarding and grasping instead of giving and receiving.

For many people, self-doubt is enemy number one, but it too is an offshoot of self-centeredness. Where do the doubts originate? Nobody can make you feel inferior, less competent, or less able unless your own mind accepts and affirms it. Doubts are powered by your own thoughts as memories of past failures creep in, making you susceptible to negative influences from outside sources.

Perhaps by now you're asking, what about superstar athletes and CEOs who have out-of-control egos? While fear is, I believe, the primary obstacle we all face, it does not stop everyone. Fear can be incredibly motivating; it is a powerful energy, after all. The hitch is that for most of us, fear stops us from performing with freedom and passion. This book is about achieving extraordinary success, which includes a balanced, fulfilling life. An ego out of control severely inhibits that.

Self-Centered Versus Self-Aware

Before continuing any further, we should differentiate between the self-centeredness that blocks progress and the self-care and self-awareness that develops and nurtures your evolution. In our discussion, self-centeredness is a trait that leads to uncertainty, frustration, and anxiety, because it prevents us from seeing the whole picture. It relies on seemingly logical thinking, the type that says, "I failed last time, I'll fail again." Extraordinary achievement, in contrast, uses the imagination to see possibilities beyond our experiences and knowledge. It's often based on what might be considered irrational thinking, the kind that allows us to send a man to the moon, break world records, or beat more talented opponents.

Self-centeredness is a nearsightedness that can't see beyond failures and limits and instead is filled with limiting thoughts of who you can't be or what you can't do. The broader view of self-awareness, however, brings options that aren't limited to your experience or rational mind. Self-awareness is the wisdom that knows your true self and your vast potential and that views your circumstances objectively as feedback to continually learn and grow.

The difference between the self-centered person and the self-aware person is in how each individual thinks and views the world. The self-centered person's thoughts are limited and insecure, moving toward doubt and fear. For example, a self-centered person walks out of a meeting that went badly and tells herself she is a poor public speaker and will never be comfortable addressing a group. She looks at her peers and thinks, "If only I were more like them, I'd be able to show everyone how good I am and get ahead." She is surprised when a colleague compliments her on something she said during her presentation. She assumes that the colleague is only being nice and will probably talk about her behind her back. When the next meeting is scheduled, she dreads walking into the room. Self-centeredness is the veil that covers our ability to see possibilities, disconnects us from others, and makes us self-conscious.

Meanwhile, a self-aware person might have come out of the same rough meeting having experienced a similar disappointment in her performance. She looks around and realizes that those who handled the situation better took more time to prepare themselves. She understands that she'll have to do the same to effectively present her ideas. Open to the compliments of her colleagues, she uses them to reaffirm her belief that her insightful ideas just require more work on the back end to be received as she intends them. When the next meeting is scheduled, she is confident. The self-aware person sees more options; there is no failure, only feedback.

Fully Engaged, Yet Unattached

Self-centeredness is a concern for self that creates a disconnect from the performance—another entity to worry about. In the best moments, when performance is fluid and perfect, there is no concern for self; you merge into the action, and your worries and self-consciousness fade away. The dancer becomes the dance. Instead, when self-concern materializes in a performance, all the doubts and limitations emerge also. Self-concern wants to see the whole picture but can't see beyond the self.

There is an important distinction to understand as we proceed, and that is the benefit of being the observer in a performance, unattached to the outcome. When you can perform with no needs, worries, or concerns—as if you were an unbiased observer—then there is freedom. It's powerful. Peak experiences, from which peak performance is derived, stem from this complete absorption into the performance. It's as if you disappear into the action and yet remain unattached.

Timothy Gallwey, author of *The Inner Game of Tennis*, says that at moments of peak performance, "the mind becomes one with what the body is doing, and the unconscious or automatic functions are working without interference from thoughts. The concentrated mind has no room for thinking how well the body is doing, much less of the how-tos of the doing. When the player is in this state of concentration, he is really into the game; he is at one with the racket, ball, and stroke; he discovers his true potential." When you're in that ideal performance state in which time slows down and everything flows, there are very few thoughts, and the ones that exist are productive and resourceful, not concerned about yourself at all.

Chapter 5 develops the theme of how to be the observer, detached from the outcome but absorbed in the performance.

 ## The Ego and the Obsession with Outcome

The problem of the ego comes when we place our identity in external success that we can't control. It's an easy thing to do, especially for high achievers with formidable goals. Goals are highly motivational, but they can enslave us if we're not careful. Obsession with the outcome of a goal is the lifeline for the ego. It's a fine line, because extraordinary achievement calls for extraordinary desire, intense training, and laser focus. The most productive course is to direct our desires and focus to the present moment. The ego, however, is always concerned about the future. The best coaches and athletes, I've found, don't talk about winning as much as performing, training, and improving.

One of the aspects of self-actualization, as Maslow said, is to "recognize our ego defenses and be able to drop them when appropriate." For our purposes, ego is that defensive self-regard, that part

, the mind that clings to temporary pleasures, disregarding the reason you want those things. (The part of the mind that's uberconfident—what we desperately want—is not the same.) The ego can never have enough; it constantly compares itself with others, wanting more possessions, more money, more achievements, more admiration. It makes you self-conscious because it relies on the external world to validate itself. When you have fancy adornments or status or medals, you can look at them and tell yourself, "I am somebody; I've got this or I've done that." You can project yourself into various roles and wear the masks that cover up who you really are.

The biggest [obstacle to peak performance] for most performers, in my thirty years, is overanalysis—the tendency, for the right reasons, to start overanalyzing things, which interferes with having a total focus when performing. The second-biggest obstacle is caring too much, getting almost obsessed with having to be successful—caring so much that it interferes.

—Dr. Cal Botterill

The ego is attached to what Stanford professor Caroline Dweck describes as a fixed mind-set, in which you're always in danger of being measured by a failure. A failure can define you in a permanent way. The idea of trying hard and still failing—of leaving yourself without excuses—is the worst fear of the fixed mind-set. According to Dweck, many people believe that great geniuses are not supposed to need to put forth effort, and if you try and fail, it robs you of all your excuses.

When your ego takes over, you become firmly attached to the outcome of your performance and the circumstances leading up to the performance.

As a result, you struggle to handle failure. Dean Smith, who coached Michael Jordan, among others, said, "It's an absolute necessity for a leader to be able to handle losing. The bigger a person's job, the more losses he or she will have, and the more costly they will be." The ego cannot handle losing, because its identity is totally based on outcomes, and losing is a direct blow to the validation-seeking ego.

The three parts of the mind that arm the monster, the Critic, the Trickster, and the Monkey Mind, are all fed by the ego, and vice versa. The ego's attachment to the outcome (rather than staying in the present) ignites the process of doubt and fear.

The Critic and Its Constant State of Reaction

The ego powers the Critic, which is attached to our circumstances. Since the ego relies on successful outcomes for its identity, it's always looking at the events leading up to the outcomes to see if we're on track. That's the Critic. If it looks as if we're getting closer to our goals, we feel good; if it looks as if we're further away, we feel bad. Even though we don't have all the information, we act as if we do, judging each circumstance, labeling it good or bad, and reacting emotionally to it. In truth, nothing is "either good or bad," as Shakespeare wrote, "but thinking makes it so." In constantly reacting to the outer world, we're not able to focus on what needs to be done in the present.

If we absolutely have to win a game, get a hit, or make a killer presentation, then we become attached not only to the outcome but also to the circumstances surrounding our efforts toward achieving that goal. Everything becomes good or bad, helpful or hurtful, taking us closer to or further away from our target. We become simply reactionary beings, bouncing between events in our lives like a pinball, high one moment and low the next, depending on how we perceived the moment to be.

In our attachment to circumstances, fear takes hold, because when we really want something, we fear we may not get it. Likewise, when we have something, we fear we may lose it. What will happen to me if I lose this game? If I fail? If my boss or coach drops me from the team? When we absolutely have to have something over which we are not in full control, we become a servant to it. We lose a bit of ourselves and become fully at the mercy of our desires. Each circumstance becomes a barometer displaying who we are and what we've achieved. We get enslaved by our performance. Or you could say, we get enslaved by the moment-to-moment feedback on how our performance is going.

Most people live in a constant state of reaction and thus struggle to reach their goals. Wisdom and insight are often lost due to the emotions of the moment. You may constantly oppose hardship, but the fact is, the effort to overcome adversity trains you, molds you, and teaches you. Pain leads to change. Say, for example, you're cut from the team or you lose your job. Bad, right? Maybe, but is it possible that this event will turn out to be not only good but also the best thing for you? Michael Jordan was famously cut from his high school basketball team and went on to be the best player in the world. Getting cut lit a fire under him, and he began getting up before school to practice. He trained harder than ever. Had he not been cut, it's doubtful he would have trained as hard as he did. When you lose your job, there could be a much better job waiting for you. Still, it's human nature to react negatively to what appears to be bad. In every situation, in fact, your mind can judge occurrences as negative. Even in the best situations, things can always be better. By the same token, you may say, "Yes, this is good, but how long will it last?" Lance Armstrong, seven-time winner of the Tour de France, said he won the Tour *because* of, not despite, his cancer. It gave him perspective, helped him focus in the present, and taught him how to live.

The Critic in all of us is attached to our circumstances, continually evaluating each event and reacting emotionally to that evaluation. If we can learn to let go of the judgment, then we can see more clearly, learn, and grow. When we react emotionally to a setback, or a rude person, or a flat tire, we know the Critic is at work, trying to pull us into the immediate but unimportant external event with which we were confronted. The crux of the matter, thankfully, is not our first reaction, but what we do next.

When we let logic and rational thought override purpose, we give fuel to the Critic. When, instead, we resist letting temporary setbacks and failures take us too far out of the present moment, and we acknowledge that it could be the best thing for us, then we've got options. We constantly resist what we think is bad, even though we often don't know if it really is until much later, if ever. Every situation carries with it learning and wisdom to be gained if we can be present enough in our adversity to see clearly. Life cannot teach us if we rebel against the teacher.

The Trickster and Its Deceptive Voice

One of the looming barriers to withholding judgment is that little voice in one's head that whispers those lies, stirring up the doubts and anxiety. Because we are attached to our circumstances, we don't immediately reject the lies of the Trickster. We let them hang around, gather strength from other negative thoughts, and convince us that, yes, it's true, we are not able to earn a promotion, pass the next test, or defeat the upcoming opponents. We get tricked into arguing for our limitations. The Trickster is the voice that whispers the doubts and fears that take hold because of the constant judgments of the Critic.

The Trickster is so deceptive because it sounds so logical. It's always got the facts to support its criticisms. It knows all your failures and how to push your buttons, and it pushes them whenever it can. After years of listening to the lies whispered in your ears, it's natural to start believing some of them. The Trickster tells you things such as, "You're not the kind of person who becomes president, or the kind of person who makes an all-star team." "You always screw up in that situation." "It's not worth even trying; you won't get it."

Perhaps the greatest power of the Trickster lies in its ability to diminish our self-worth. High achievers, with their perfectionist tendencies, are often exceedingly hard on themselves. This need to succeed is a curse as much as a blessing. In our intense drive for success, we may belittle ourselves when we lose or perform poorly. Instead of motivating us to get better, the Trickster makes us feel bad about ourselves. Performance coach Dr. Ken Ravizza states: "Perfectionism is one of the biggest things I run into, especially with Olympic and professional athletes. That's one of the biggest obstacles. I think one of the other things is that athletes [and coaches] tend to personalize it. You throw bad BP [batting practice]; therefore, you're a terrible person—'What's wrong with me?'" We beat ourselves up for our failures instead of learning from them, so we get depressed, and self-rejection becomes the central issue.

Self-rejection is a symptom of still a larger issue. In our preoccupation with self (self-concern), we see all our limitations and automatically move toward them. Anxiety emerges, which unchecked leads toward self-rejection, fear, and possibly panic. Self-centeredness is the larger issue, the root cause. When we fail in some event, it's often a trigger for the downward slide. Seattle sport psychologist David Coppel calls this sequence of events the D-slide:

> The D-slide begins when failure goes from *disappointment*, "I should have done it and wasn't able to," to feeling *devastated*, where it spreads out to involve more areas you perceive you can't do, to feeling *defeated*, which means I'm helpless to change it, and finally you feel *defective*: "There's something wrong with me." Some people travel down the slide quickly, or in a different order, but after a while, a lot of people go straight from disappointment to defective. For those people, it increases self-consciousness, and every error adds to the bag of feeling bad about yourself, which isn't going to help performance.

Attachment to the outcome creates insecurity: from here it's a slippery slope to self-rejection. Say, for example, you lose a big sale. You're disappointed, a natural reaction, but because you wanted the sale so badly, you became attached to it and felt devastated when you didn't get it. The Critic says, "This is really bad," and the Trickster steps in and reminds you of all your other failures and then projects more in the future. Now you're starting to feel like a failure.

If, however, when you initially set the goal of getting the sale, you had focused on the qualities you needed as a salesperson, you would have had a much better chance of making the sale. Two principal factors in high performance are the ability to be present and to focus on the process. The Trickster, the Critic, and the Monkey Mind (more on that component in a moment) all take you out of the present. They continually pull you to the past, whether it's five years ago or thirty seconds ago. In the past, of course, lie all your failures.

Yale professor Henri Nouwen calls the negative voices in our heads one of our utmost struggles: "These negative voices are so loud and so persistent that it is easy to believe them. That's the great trap. It is the trap of self-rejection. Over the years, I have come to realize that the greatest trap in our life is not success, popularity, or power, but self-rejection." Perhaps for Nouwen, the affluenza virus is fueled by self-rejection. Self-rejection, I believe, is fueled by making ourselves the center of our universe. As philosopher Henry David Thoreau said, "The mass of men lead lives of quiet desperation." The despair of self-rejection is a real obstacle empowered by our self-centeredness, which fuels the Trickster.

The Trickster is powerful and deceptive because of our attachment to the past. With every failure filed away, it's a short step to relive past failures, one eye on the future and one eye on the past, ignoring the present.

The Monkey Mind and Its Overanalysis

From the minute we wake up to the moment we go to sleep, the mind churns out an endless stream of thoughts. Even in sleep, the mind is sorting, filing, and dreaming of the thoughts we've had throughout the day. The vast majority of these thoughts are about ourselves and everything that affects us. Unfortunately, so many are unproductive or negative. These thoughts tend to repeat themselves, day after day, and turn into beliefs about what's possible and what's not, about who we are, and about who we can or probably won't become. This cluttered, negative state of consciousness is the Monkey Mind. The Trickster and the Critic often ignite the Monkey Mind, because as we listen to the doubts and fears, and as we judge our circumstances as good or bad, we open ourselves up to endless chatter and analysis. Analysis is important to learning and growth, but it becomes an obstacle when we can't turn off the self-talk, especially during performance.

We give our thoughts so little recognition because we have thousands of them every day. The emotions of the Critic have ample power to drive our behaviors because of the thoughts that create those emotions. Where our thoughts go, so go our desires, our emotions, and our destiny.

We have so many thoughts that we're no longer aware of them. They've just become a part of us. Charlie Maher, performance coach for the Cleveland Indians, says that this is our biggest obstacle: "Primarily it's the athletes' inability to catch their use of unproductive thoughts, unproductive ways of thinking about the situation they're in. That translates into 'What if this happens?' 'What if that happens?' 'I'm not doing well right now.' The more technical term is *fusing with their language*. They let their language take on a reality of its own."

He describes how it affects professional baseball players: "Fusing with their language is thinking a thought and creating a reality— 'What if this happens?' and 'I don't know if I can get through this inning.' So, they're creating a reality, when the real reality is there's a hitter, there's a catcher, and there may be men on base. So, when you translate that, they lose their focus, lose their composure, and become tense." As with Maher's baseball players, we've all created these stories throughout our lives, distorted by negativity, mostly without realizing it. It doesn't matter what our actual talents are if our perceptions are creating a story cluttered with negative thoughts.

Say you've been struggling in your job. The thought comes that you're not good at what you do. By itself, that thought is powerless, but if you focus on that thought and give it merit by letting it stay in your mind, other thoughts will come along to verify it. Soon the premise that you are not talented makes perfect sense, because you also failed at this and that and those other things. Now the thought becomes reality, whereas had you dismissed it initially and replaced it with a positive thought, you would have had a much better chance of stemming the tide of negativity.

Jim Fannin works with world-class athletes and executives, teaching them how to perform with poise under pressure. One of the most important things he does with his clients is teach them to have fewer, more efficient thoughts. "With no exceptions, of more than 150 professional athletes I've coached, I put all of them on a mental diet," he says. It's no different at home or at the office: without knowing how to stop the endless stream of thoughts, we'll fall into the trap of negativity. Self-actualization, the ability to live fully and passionately, comes from finding a way to get clarity amid the chaos, as you'll see in Chapter 5.

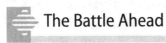

The Battle Ahead

Speaking at a commencement ceremony, professor David Foster Wallace discussed our sea of thoughts: "As I'm sure you guys know by now, it is extremely difficult to stay alert and attentive, instead of getting hypnotized by the constant monologue inside your own head, which may be happening right now. Teaching you how to think is actually shorthand for a much deeper, more serious idea: learning how to think really means learning how to exercise some control over how and what you think. It means being conscious and aware enough to choose what you pay attention to and to choose how you construct meaning from experience."

Meaning is tied to perception, and perception grows from attention. A thought has power only by what you give it, and you give an unproductive thought power when you let it linger in your mind. The longer it stays, the more unproductive thoughts will follow. Soon you get attached to those thoughts, and the thoughts become one with you. The thinker becomes the thought.

Attachment to your thoughts is a stubborn obstacle to your growth and performance. Without being able to stop the constant flow of thoughts, so many of which are negative or useless, your goals get buried. You form limiting beliefs based on wrong information. Life becomes one frustration after another. When you learn to slow down the constant flow of thoughts and weed out the ones that are not productive, brighter thoughts come—more opportunistic, more imaginative, and more powerful. It's not life and difficulties that you must conquer; it's the thoughts that become the monster within you.

In the battle for your heart, your thoughts are crucial. Every day, you wake up with dreams to be realized and amazing experiences that await, if you master the ability to direct your thoughts. Your mind, with its predisposition toward self-centeredness, will lean toward limitations, be self-conscious and attached to the needs of the ego. The good news is that it's not an impossible barrier to overcome. Throughout history people have learned to direct their thoughts, focus their desires, and see the world closer to what it truly is, with all its opportunities. As you'll see in upcoming chapters, you can learn to direct your thoughts toward powerful concepts, such as love, wisdom, and courage. As you develop empowering habits, you'll begin to reap the benefits of a clear mind and an unburdened heart. You'll learn how to stay completely in the moment, unconcerned about the outcome or how you'll be viewed if you fail.

Key Points for Chapter 2

- ◆ Fear of failure is the chief obstacle to freedom and peak performance.
- ◆ Our natural preoccupation with ourselves and the attachment to our past that it brings is the root cause of this fear.
- ◆ This preoccupation leads to past failures and self-consciousness, which fuels the ego, which is always searching for external validation.
- ◆ In our intense desire to succeed, we get attached to the outcome of our goals, but we can't control them, so we become needy.
- ◆ The mind has three parts that continually want to live in the past and future: the Trickster, the Critic, and the Monkey Mind, which remind us of our failures, judge every circumstance, and fill the mind with negatives.
- ◆ We've never been taught how to manage our minds, and thus doubts and anxiety have more power than they should.

Follow-Up Questions and Activities

- Practice observing your thoughts. How do your thoughts affect you?
- How often do you find your mind in the past or future?
- Do you find yourself getting caught up in life's trivial setbacks—being cut off in traffic, a parking ticket, a rude comment—or are you able to consistently rise above your circumstances and stay focused on what matters most?
- Do you tend to overanalyze things?
- Are you able to stop the constant flow of thoughts in your mind when you need to?

The Quest for Fearlessness

Three Pillars of Extraordinary Success

Love is the triumph of imagination over intelligence.

—H. L. Mencken

On July 15, 2007, Lewis Gordon Pugh stepped purposefully into his quarters of the Russian ship. As he put on his Speedo swimsuit, he thought of the danger that lay ahead. The *NS Yamal* was berthed at ninety degrees north latitude in the arctic circle. The nuclear-powered icebreaker swayed in the pitch-black water measuring −1.7 degrees Celcius through which Pugh would soon find himself swimming. Fear gripped him. Three years earlier he had embarked on a journey that, in the next half hour, would change his life forever. Professor Tim Noakes, a sport scientist and doctor, entered the chamber to outfit him with his core body temperature gauge. Other than the armed guards on the lookout for hungry polar bears, Noakes was the only person who could stop the swim. Pugh was going for a world-record attempt at swimming one kilometer at the geographic north pole, fully exposed to the ice water.

When a person is swimming in freezing waters, the brain goes into slow-motion mode. "It doesn't think clearly or respond normally," Noakes explained. "If the swimmer's core body temperature reaches a certain point, there is no way to get it back. The swimmer will be swimming one moment and be sinking toward the ocean bottom the next. I had to make sure he never reached that point." Pugh's life was in Noakes's hands. "If there was any way I could have turned back, I would have," Pugh remarked. "I looked into Tim's eyes and saw fear, which I had never seen before. His hands shook as he was outfitting me with the temperature gauge."

There was reason to fear. Scientists around the world said it couldn't be done, that it would be life-threatening. Dr. Tim Noakes was one of the few sport scientists who said it was possible. And now that the swim was imminent, Noakes was scared. Maybe they were right. Three weeks before his attempt at the north pole, Pugh trained at a glacial lake in Norway. The water was three degrees Celsius, significantly warmer than the waters of the arctic circle. The farthest he was able to get, however, was only about six hundred meters.

Two days before the epic swim, Pugh and his team (he had a twenty-nine member crew) decided to do another trial run. Results were disastrous. He had not even completed a third of the distance before pain overtook him and he had to abort. The cells in his hands had burst. "I can't describe to you what it was like," he said. "It felt as if someone had been stomping up and down on my hands for hours." British explorer Sir Ranulph Fiennes had attempted to retrieve his sled from those same icy waters years earlier and lost most of his fingers to frostbite after only three minutes exposure.

After the two failed test swims, Pugh's doubts were so massive that he became depressed. With his entire crew counting on him, not to mention the worldwide press calling each day for updates, the pressure was mounting. Nevertheless, Pugh was a man on a mission, as this swim was bigger than he was: to do what he was attempting at the north pole, where the water is normally frozen over by meters of ice, would bring attention to the devastating effects of global warming.

A couple of major setbacks and the fear of death were not going to stop him from giving it his best shot. Despite his intense fear, Pugh went through with his bid to swim one kilometer in waters that would kill most people in less than a minute. This time, success! The question is, how did he overcome his fear, especially after two major failures?

There seemed to be a quantum leap that got Pugh from his test-run failures, which left him engulfed in fear, to the confidence and focus that allowed him to conquer the impossible. Obviously, he did not become stronger, faster, or cold-blooded in two days. The difference wasn't physical. There had to be something that clicked, that changed everything.

Filled with fear and doubt just before his epic swim, Pugh had an enormous challenge in front of him. He knew not only that he was about to endure incredible pain but also that he could die doing so. In those two dark days, he had some serious and difficult work to do. There were some looming questions: Could he believe in himself when logic said he would fail? Could he focus completely in the moment and not let distracting thoughts settle in? Could he overcome the fear of death?

In the pursuit of our most difficult goals and dreams, we all must face our doubts and fears. Fear is potent partly because of the trouble we have in pinpointing its origins, making it harder to address. As you familiarize yourself with how your mind works, you can learn to embrace your fear and not be frozen by it.

This book describes a way of life, a model for thinking and perceiving the world. It's going to take some work, however, to see how your mind is engineered. We've covered some of the pitfalls already: how the ego makes you needy, the Trickster deceives you, the Critic fuels emotional instability, and the Monkey Mind scatters your energy.

In this chapter we'll delve into how Pugh won his inner battle and how you can do the same. We'll probe the ways that love, wisdom, and courage teach us to lead with the heart, expand our vision, and be fully present. When the pressure is most intense, and your greatest fears are possible, there must be something greater to overcome it—something beyond your goal, beyond winning, beyond, perhaps, even death.

The Road to Fearlessness

One thing that didn't change in the two days between Pugh's crushing failure and stunning success was fear. After his second failed test swim, he thought, "At best, I will lose a few fingers; at worst, I will die." He desperately wanted to turn back and give up. It was not until the moment he stepped out onto the sea ice that his fear turned into aggression. How was he able to overcome his fear, depression, and doubt?

Before we examine *how* he did it, it may help to look at *why* he would do it. He asked himself that very question over and over: "So, what pushes somebody? I'm not a lunatic; I'm not a madman. I'm a lawyer. I have a lot of experience in swimming. What pushes somebody to sail all the way to the geographic north pole, seven days of sailing, and stand there on the ice, and take the jump, when even the experts say you could very well kill yourself?"

Why would anyone purposely risk death? It seems there are three possible reasons someone may do so:

+ For a purpose beyond the individual (some cause, or to save or help others)
+ To feel alive in a way that can be experienced only when pushing oneself to the limit, perhaps close to death
+ Lack of concern for oneself, at least in that moment

Fear, as with all seven basic emotions (see Chapter 5), is designed to help us. Fear protects us from danger and helps us focus. The problem occurs when our emotions get out of control. There is so much energy in fear that it can be crippling. Pugh was able to use the energy from fear to empower him. When he stepped out onto the ice at the north pole, a sense of confidence and intensity came over him. Something clicked when he felt the bitter cold: "I was in a totally different zone. I walked off the ship, and somehow, for the first time ever, I felt

> What animates [mountain] climbers is not a death wish, but a life wish, a desire to truly live—fully, intensely, completely. I have never met a group of people more truly alive—physically, emotionally, intellectually, spiritually. Rather than courting danger for its own sake, they do so as a means of deepening and enriching their experience.
>
> —Nicholas O'Connell, *Beyond Risk: Conversations with Climbers*

so confident that this thing was going to happen." His "self" faded to the background as he became so connected with the mission and his team that he risked his very life to accomplish his purpose.

What Pugh did was connect with something bigger than himself. The swim was his way of using his gifts to make a positive difference in the world, in something he truly cared about. Pugh found something that was so compelling—the devastation of global warming—that he was willing to give his life for it. In doing this, he found a way to truly live.

Absolute Fullness of Life

To truly live is to seek self-actualization, according to Abraham Maslow. It's the final level, he said, of personal development. Some key characteristics of self-actualization are to have a cause greater than yourself and to connect with your true self and with others. There is a Greek word that describes this phenomenon: Zoë.

Zoë is the state of being possessed of vitality, with absolute fullness of life, real and genuine, active and vigorous. It's the full potential of your inner life, the generator of beauty and passion so intense that the moments have a sacred quality to them, detached from every obstacle, doubt, and fear.

Zoë encompasses love, wisdom, and courage, the three of them intimately interconnected—you can't experience one fully without some of the other two. When you experience all three together, while pursuing your unique gifts, Zoë unfolds in sacred moments.

To pursue Zoë is to lead with your heart (love), expand your vision (wisdom), and be fully present (courage).

Leading with the heart is to develop the self-awareness needed to live with passion and be your true self.

Expanding your vision is to see more of reality—beyond yourself; to have a purpose beyond your goals, be a part of something greater than yourself, and continually expand your beliefs to drive your growth.

To be fully present is to be fully engaged in the moment; to see beauty and have a clear mind and unburdened heart, with no needs or self-concern in that moment. It takes courage to be fully present, but when you are, you set the stage to perform with poise under pressure.

To continually lead with your heart, expand your vision, and be fully present is to seek self-mastery. Mastery is the pursuit of personal development. It's not dependent on outcome, although outcomes become more fruitful as mastery is increased. Personal development seeks self-awareness in order to learn life's lessons. By definition, personal development is about growth, and so mastery is the pursuit of self-awareness and growth. Mastery is always seeking to have the inner peace, confidence, and heightened awareness that come with being fully present.

When you are fully present in performance, five characteristics emerge: swagger, focus, relaxation, enjoyment, and discipline. These five markers give you the best chance to succeed and win. (We will study these markers in more depth in Chapter 8.) This is where many athletes or goal-oriented people stop; they just want to win— but that's a mistake. You're missing out on absolute fullness of life when external success is the only thing driving you forward. *Fullness of life is always in the present moment, whereas success is always a past or future thing.*

We want the medal, fast car, big raise, or first-class vacation because we think it will provide us with an extraordinary experience. Usually when we think of great experiences, we think in terms of sports, music, art, or travel, but experience is dependent on the experiencer. We have it within us to create the conditions that lead to great experiences, which in turn lead to great performances.

Dreams Versus Goals

The words *dreams* and *goals* are often used interchangeably, but here we differentiate. Goals are external outcomes that are not in your full control: get a raise, win a match, hit .300, become CEO. Dreams are feelings. We set goals in order to get the feelings we want. Winning a championship is amazing because of the feeling. It's not the trophy or medal that does it; that's just the symbol. What we really want are ways to integrate our gifts and passion to feel truly alive— that's living our dreams.

Dawn Staley was a professional basketball player who won three gold medals in the Olympic Games. In Doug Newburg's book *The Most Important Lesson No One Ever Taught Me*, Staley describes her perspective in preparation for the Olympics:

> Winning the gold medal is my goal, not my dream. My dream is about playing to win as often as possible with and against the best women basketball players in the world. Winning the gold medal as a goal gives me some direction, but my dream is something I need to live every day. And I'm doing that each time I play to win. . . . When I'm playing to win, that's when I feel resonance. If I win, that's great. I want

to win, and having the gold medal as my goal forces me to play to win. But what I love to do, what my dream is, is to play to win.

Zoë captures those dreams. And it goes beyond. Zoë connects us with our true selves and integrates us with the Zoë in others. When the monster of self is at full strength, it is filled with fear, self-rejection, and doubt. When we are focused on Zoë, however, our pursuit of love, wisdom, and courage becomes passion, purpose, and presence. Every day we wake up with the choice of where to focus our thoughts, attention, and desires. If we so choose, we can focus on Zoë with its three pillars of excellence: love, wisdom, and courage. In this pursuit a positive energy emerges with five key characteristics: a swagger, focus, relaxation, enjoyment, and discipline. When this positive energy intersects with your gifts, a powerful frequency materializes: resonance. Resonance is the energy that comes when your gifts and loves are challenged in a meaningful way. Truly extraordinary experiences result. Along the way we are able to perform our best in whatever we do, with poise under pressure. To pursue Zoë is to pursue a way of life, one that seeks self-mastery and the resulting passion, purpose, and poise it brings. See Figure 3.1.

Love: Lead with Your Heart

When you lead with your heart, so much is possible. Leading with the heart starts by pursuing the self-awareness necessary to learn how to develop your *true self*. Your true self feels, lives, and competes congruently and powerfully. Leading with your heart is also to be *true to yourself* in order to unveil the passion inside.

Figure 3.1 **The Path to Zoë**

Tanya Streeter is a free diver—think pearl diver—who dived 525 feet straight down into the ocean, on a single breath, to set the world record. She was a world champion, but that title did not define her. "It's what I did," she says, "but it is not who I am, at all." For Streeter, diving offered a place in which to retreat and forget her troubles and, especially, a way to grow, gain confidence, and learn about herself. She used her gift to increase her sense of self so she could come back to shore and confront the challenges in her personal life.

She adds, "I didn't find a cure for cancer or walk on Mars or anything; it really wasn't that great. But in my own world it was what I needed to do to travel to the edge of myself and look back and say, all right, it's enough and it's OK, because I achieved my goal in the course of doing it. . . . I thoroughly believe that human beings have an innate desire to understand who they are. I believe through my experiences that you have to travel to the absolute edge of yourself physically, mentally, emotionally, and, in my case, financially to be able to look back and see everything you're made of. With every training dive I ever did, I was pushing to the edge of myself."

Streeter's experiences in free diving taught her how strong she could be, and that lesson helped her in the rest of her life. She states, "I'm just so enormously blessed that I had that sport and that aquatic environment [she grew up in the Cayman Islands] to be able to discover that about myself, so that I can get on with the rest of my life. I've accepted it all [my insecurities]. It's not as if I've got over it; it's a case of accepting it and knowing how strong you can be if you want to. I think it's the most valuable lesson you can learn."

> Success, like happiness, cannot be pursued; it must ensue, and it only does so as the unintended side-effect of one's personal dedication to a cause greater than oneself.
>
> —Viktor Frankl, holocaust survivor and author, *Man's Search for Meaning*

To be true to yourself, you must develop your sense of self. Your sense of self is your comfort with who you are as a person. Take away your money, possessions, achievements, and status, and the person who is left, the feeling of who you are then, reveals your sense of self. A strong sense of self is characterized by inner confidence and peace, with no need for bragging or being defensive. You don't need to have this or that or to win the approval of anyone. You feel good about yourself regardless of your circumstance, role, or status.

Without a strong sense of self, you'll take detours off the path of self-mastery, looking for shortcuts. There's always a nicer car, bigger house, or shinier medal that beckons to steal your heart. Where your heart is, your mind and body will follow. To be true to yourself, guide your heart toward that which is most powerful while pursuing your goals. What's most powerful is to focus on the love, wisdom, and courage that develops into passion, purpose, and poise.

Your true self sees more clearly, loves more deeply, and lives more fully. It's the greatness within you that has an ability to see beauty and to connect with others, as well as a willingness to look foolish. Your self-acceptance rises the more you can connect with who you really are, in which case you'll inspire and connect with others. This will energize your own spirit as your love toward others increases the love within yourself. When you're true to yourself and not a slave to results, you can perform with freedom.

Your heart is the part of you that contains your best self, the greatness that sometimes emerges, if only for a brief moment, but retreats when bombarded by the self-absorbed mind and instant-gratification body. To lead with your heart is to passionately pursue experience over outcome, to perform with freedom, to seek out your true self and be congruent to that part of you, to live fully, to love. Fear is powered by an inability to see beyond yourself, while love is the lens that sees the great possibilities, the bigger picture and interconnectedness of life.

Wisdom: Expand Your Vision

To be true to yourself is to accept that there is much more to life than you can see right now. So, you look to extend your vision beyond your own experiences, ideas, and skills. It takes wisdom and discipline to be true to yourself.

Expanding your vision is to pursue growth. You do that by having a purpose beyond your goals, looking to be a part of something greater than yourself, and developing beliefs that are congruent to your growth. To expand your vision is to seek wisdom by developing self-awareness and awareness of how the world in which you live works. As you develop awareness, you'll see the interconnectedness of all humanity, and you'll seek to develop powerful relationships. You'll also see the bigger picture, which helps remove the barriers of your limiting beliefs and expands what's possible in life. Your awareness will reveal the blinders of self-centeredness, pride, and ego and will show how humility and gratitude lead to extraordinary experiences.

> A grateful person is a powerful person, for gratitude generates power. All abundance is based on being grateful for what we have.
>
> **Elizabeth Kubler-Ross**, *Life Lessons*

Gratitude and humility are the foundation from which your true self emerges. As you learn and grow, you'll gain the self-awareness to challenge the beliefs that limit you and replace them with more powerful beliefs. The exemplary people Maslow studied, as detailed in Chapter 1, learned that to reach their highest goals meant to connect with others, learn from them, and help them. University of Chicago professor Mihaly Csikszentmihalyi, who has studied thousands of top performers in his research on flow and creativity, concluded, "To achieve peak performance you should have a strongly directed purpose that is not self-seeking."

When you see only yourself, your vision is too nearsighted and misses out on the energy and power of those around you. The greatness that lies within you is incomplete until it connects with something beyond you and with others around you. When that connection is made, you capture the vision of others and see further and greater things. It gives you more power to expand your beliefs and overcome the difficulties and adversities you face. The power within is your freedom of choice, to choose to see beyond your temporary needs and desires, embracing the bigger picture. First, though, you must let go of temporary things so you can get a hold of the greatness awaiting you and let your true self emerge.

Lewis Pugh swam at the north pole not for the glamour or money, but for the dying coral reefs he saw up close in his goggles— the effects of global warming. It was a purpose beyond himself that gave him the courage to face death.

Pugh's connection to his team was a major factor in his epic achievement. After his failed attempt just before the big swim, his performance coach, David Becker, took him to the front of the ship and laid out a plan:

> Your team consists of twenty-nine people from ten nations. I'm going to put one of their flags at every hundred-meter mark. The first flag will be the Norwegian flag, because that will get you into the water. [Pugh is British, a rival of Norway.] The second flag will be the Swedish flag, and then the Russian flag, and then the Canadian flag, and so on and so forth, until you get to the British flag at the end. All I want you to do is to think about those people who have sacrificed so much for you, who've inspired you so much that you're actually here today. And when you stand at the start, all I want you to think about are the Norwegians on your team. Just think about the hundred-meter mark. Please, Lewis, do

not think about doing a kilometer; you will never make it. Break that beast down into little manageable chunks, and when you get to the Norwegian flag, forget about the Norwegians and just think about the Swedes, and so on until you get to the end.

Two critical engines powered Pugh in his incredible feat: a purpose beyond himself and a strong connection to members of his team. Those two factors helped him to be fully present in the midst of extreme danger and pain. When you find a purpose that provides you with its own reward simply by the act of pursuing it, then you'll be empowered. If that purpose serves the greater good, it will provide meaning in your life. A purpose beyond yourself moves your identity from what you have and what you've achieved to affecting others; your value increases and your concern for self decreases. It attacks your insecurities by increasing your self-worth.

Jerry Kramer, the famous guard for the Green Bay Packers in their Super Bowl heyday with Vince Lombardi and Bart Starr, was asked what his motivation was for playing football. He said he played pro football for all the men who had been his teammates: "I'll tell you in a nutshell, if you can understand this: I play pro football because of Emlen Tunnell, Bill Quinlan, Dan Currie, Paul Hornung . . . ."

What Pugh did had never been done before; few people even thought it was possible, but Pugh dreamed it and achieved it. The imagination is the fuel for our greatest dreams but also for our biggest fears, and thus, it has the potential to limit or propel us, depending on its use. Every day, our thoughts are creating new beliefs or reinforcing old ones. Limiting beliefs are often barriers imposed by the Trickster, which is continually reminding us of past failures and potential future ones. When we learn how to challenge our beliefs and create ones that are more constructive, then sometimes even the impossible becomes possible.

Courage: Be Fully Present

Lewis Pugh had to be fully present in order to swim in freezing waters. He couldn't think for a second about how cold the water was, about the likelihood that most people would die in a minute or two in water that cold. To be present like that under life-and-death circumstances took a lot of courage. True courage is to be fully present *when* it matters most. To do so, we must learn to be fully present on *what* matters most.

What matters most is who you are and who you're becoming, because no matter what the circumstances in your life are, you are the one who experiences it, and you will remain after the experience is over. It requires courage to be true to yourself in a world trying to make you like everyone else. It's difficult to grow as a person when mediocrity exists all around you. When you are fully present, however, you can learn the lessons that life brings to teach you. You can gain the wisdom to live with passion and lead with your heart.

To be fully present is, as Dr. Botterill says, to have an unburdened heart and a clear mind. This is a difficult thing, to say the least, especially under pressure. If our goal is to perform extraordinarily, we need to learn how to be fully present in the most intense situations. To do that takes courage. Fear constantly wants to remember the past and project the future, but courage allows us to stay present through the fear. An unburdened heart and clear mind, one that is fully present, is the framework for poise.

Courage is love in action, the combination of wisdom (knowing how to live) and love (connecting with your true self and others) that overcomes fear so you can pursue your dreams. It's daring to look foolish so you can learn what it takes to be your best self. Then you can step into your fear and pursue the wisdom and love that will shape your character.

When you're fully present, there are no doubts or worries, no past or future, no concerns for self. Because there is no self-concern, there is also no fear. There is, in its place, vitality and fullness of life. Pugh was filled with fear in the moments before he got on the ice, but when he stepped outside, fear transformed into aggression, and his concern for self turned into a connection to his team. He was fully present and filled with life.

Love, wisdom, and courage not only are essential for overcoming fear but also are interwoven in how they do so. Pure love is fully present because it has no needs or attachments. Wisdom is the script for courage so we can be confident when we step into our fears.

The Life Diamond and the Pursuit of Zoë

Every day, we wake up with a choice: do we let our natural self-centeredness take over and lead us toward doubts and fears, or do we choose to focus on love, wisdom, and courage? If we don't make a conscious decision, we'll inevitably follow our natural inclination down the pyramid.

We covered the self-centered path toward fear in Chapter 2 and the purpose-filled path towards Zoë in this chapter. Let's see how it comes together in the Life Diamond shown in Figure 3.2.

Figure 3.2 **The Life Diamond**

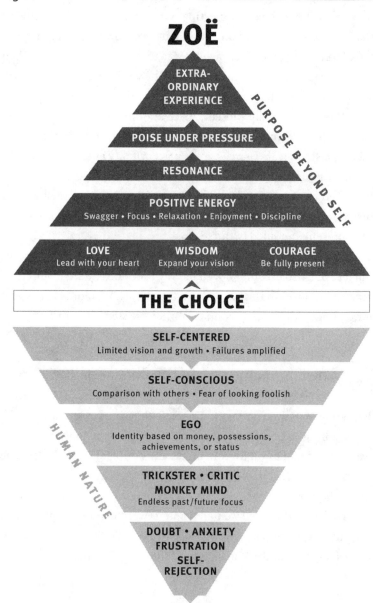

In summary, fear is overcome through love, wisdom, and courage. These three pillars are the foundation for the self-mastery that enable us to be true to ourselves and live with passion, purpose, and poise. Mastery reveals itself in our ability to be fully present with a positive energy. Earlier in this chapter, we touched on the five factors that characterize this positive energy: swagger, focus, relaxation, enjoyment, and discipline. When these five characteristics are high, we can perform with poise under pressure. The key is to be able to summon this positive energy when we need it. Thus, we want to develop an awareness of these five characteristics each day.

That positive energy, when combined with what we love and what we're good at, sets the table for what I call resonance. In physics, resonance is a state in which frequencies align. It is a dynamic force, able to produce the world's most beautiful musical harmonies at one end of the spectrum and break down barriers at the other. To be fully engaged in a great moment, with a clear mind and unburdened heart, is to experience resonance.

Resonance has moments that are so amazing they can best be described as sacred. Resonance comes most often when your gifts are challenged in a meaningful way and you're fully engaged, using those gifts. When you have resonance, your performance is effortless, and the outcome takes care of itself. Extraordinary performance is merely a subset of extraordinary experience. Poise under pressure is the by-product of resonance. The key to extraordinary performance, then, is to build on a foundation that creates the conditions for resonance.

The journey toward Zoë, absolute fullness of life, becomes more about the experience than the outcome, more about relationships than circumstances. The pursuit of Zoë is to seek out that which matters most in life. For this you seek a purpose beyond yourself, which helps you to be fearless. When the end of your life draws near, you'll look back with no regrets, with peace and fulfillment. This is Zoë.

Key Points from Chapter 3

- There are three pillars of excellence that overcome fear and form the foundation for extraordinary performance: love, wisdom, and courage.
- Love is to lead with your heart, wisdom is to expand your vision, and courage is to be fully present, all of which lead to freedom and extraordinary experiences.
- Pursuing the pillars of excellence is to pursue self-mastery.
- Five factors emerge in the form of a positive energy from this pursuit: swagger, focus, relaxation, enjoyment, and discipline.
- Resonance is to be fully present, using your gifts, challenged and connected to your true self.
- Extraordinary performance is best achieved by pursuing extraordinary experience.
- There are two critical components to being fearless: a purpose beyond yourself and connection to others.
- Zoë is absolute fullness of life, the self-actualization of those who are true to themselves.

Follow-Up Questions and Activities

- Start a journal, if you haven't already, that records how you want to live, feel, and compete.

- How have you done so far today with the five factors of performance? Did you have a sense of freedom in your work and play? What will it take to get that tomorrow?
- What sort of growth choices can you make that will expand your vision? Make a choice to put yourself in new situations in which you were previously uncomfortable. Can you lose your self-consciousness amid the discomfort?
- Consider what it means to feel resonance. When you're in the midst of the work or sport you love, what leads you to resonance? What takes it away?
- What does it mean for you to pursue absolute fullness of life?

Code of the Samurai

The Triumph of Mastery over Ego

A warrior considers it his foremost concern to keep death in mind at all times, every day and every night. . . . As long as you keep death in mind at all times, you will fulfill the ways of loyalty, avoid myriad evils and calamities, be physically sound and healthy, and live a long life. What is more, your character will improve and your virtue will grow.

—Taira Shigesuke, written four hundred years ago in a guide for young samurai

In Chapter 1 we discussed the trap of a materialistic society and how it deceptively distances us from our true selves. In Chapter 2 we looked at the root cause of fear, which is self-centeredness, the myopic lens through which we view the world. Chapter 3 presented the solution to self-centeredness, which is having love, wisdom, and courage. Now we'll see how a group of people lived by a code encapsulating those three virtues and how that enabled them to be fearless.

In our youth- and beauty-oriented culture, our lives are a constant battle against death, fighting it every step of the way. In doing so, we give up a lot. We lose a bit of ourselves each day as we give in to our fears and let instant gratification pacify the desires of the ego, burying our deep need to be our true selves. The ego latches onto anything that will give us some sort of quantifiable identity, and then it takes over our lives as we become enslaved to our goals and lose our freedom.

The real sin of the ego is not self-centeredness per se. The sin is in what it leads to: carelessness, limited vision, arrogance to cover up our feelings of lack, indifference (because of our ignorance), self-consciousness, and attachment—all of which fuel our doubt and fear.

The path toward Zoë lies in removing what's not you—the doubts, the fear, and the affluenza virus to which they cling—and finding the power inherent in love, wisdom, and courage that leads to a fearless life.

The Paradox of the Samurai

In feudal Japan, samurai warriors ruled the land. (Although they were the ruling class, most samurai were servants to higher-ranking samurai.) They were legendary for their loyalty, self-discipline, and commitment to honor. The samurai lived by an unwritten code of ethics known as Bushido, which means "Way of the warrior." Their way was to place virtue and character above all else. The code, as with this book, was based largely on three values: love, wisdom, and courage. In love, they served; in wisdom, they saw the impermanence of life; in courage, they put honor and integrity over material rewards. The framework for their training was to prepare each day to fight to the death. In order to be fearless in battle, the warrior had to be prepared to die.

This is not an easy picture to imagine in our pampered North American lives. While much of the world lives in poverty, we eat at fast-food restaurants, get movies delivered to our homes, play golf on the weekends, and are always looking to be entertained. Entertainment is a multibillion-dollar industry that capitalizes on our ever-increasing needs for pleasure.

The samurai, on the other hand, found pleasure in improvement, freedom in discipline, and love in service to others. While North America's professional athletes may be known as much for cheating as for performing, the samurai had no need for the money, status, or possessions that cheating may bring. In their preparation to die each day, the samurai focused daily on that which was most important: their spirit.

> This is the essence of Bushido. In order to master this essence, you must die anew, every morning and every night. If you continually preserve the state of death in everyday life, you will understand the essence of Bushido. Then you will gain freedom in Bushido.
>
> —Tsunetomo Yamamoto, samurai

 ## The Spirit of Mastery

The path toward mastery lies within the three pillars of love (lead with your heart), wisdom (expand your vision), and courage (be fully present). Self-mastery is the quest of how to live true to yourself, seeking to expand your vision in order to grow, and gaining the discipline to live in the present. Mastery increases confidence in yourself and decreases concern for yourself, both of which help you to be fully engaged in the moment. With a strong sense of self, we are not enslaved by our performance; we are opened up to beauty, wisdom, and sacred moments.

Every day, no matter where you are, wisdom calls out. To seek self-mastery is to hear that call and take the path devoid of the normal pleasures, instant gratifications, and admiring cheers from the crowd. This path is isolated and difficult. To be great, there is a price to be paid, and it must be paid in advance. The cost of greatness is the blood, tears, and loneliness that come from putting everything on the line as you shoot for your dreams and goals where you knowingly are exposed to the risk of public failure. It's the willingness to sacrifice what seems like everything in order to gain . . . perhaps nothing except experience, learning, and growth.

Mastery builds skills that empower every individual and business, such as creativity and problem solving. Mastery provides the most powerful foundation

> The most important trait of survivors is a "non-self-conscious individualism," or a strongly directed purpose that is not self-seeking. People who have that quality are bent on doing their best in all circumstances, yet they are not concerned primarily with advancing their own interests. Because they are intrinsically motivated in their actions, they are not easily disturbed by external threats.
>
> —Mihaly Csikszentmihalyi, Ph.D., from his book *Flow*, describing those who've succeeded with the most adversity under pressure

for both because it confronts one of the biggest obstacles that lie in the way: the ego. The ego, attached to instant gratification and external rewards, opposes mastery. Every day, we are confronted with negativity and a mind that wants to live in the past, project the future, and constantly react to every circumstance.

> Mastering others is strength. Mastering yourself makes you fearless.
>
> —Lau-tzu

To be creative and find solutions, we must have a clear mind, with no need to react nor threats to defend against. The ideas come when we are fully present, predominantly positive, and not living in a constant state of reaction (precisely the opposite work of the Trickster, Critic, and Monkey Mind). Everything we do in the quest for mastery largely comes down to the ability to be fully present in the moment.

It may help to look at self-mastery and ego in comparison in order to get a better grasp of the characteristics of each. See the sidebar comparison of mastery and ego on the following page.

 ## The Renewing of Your Mind

As you pursue love, wisdom, and courage, you will learn how to be true to yourself. In this endeavor, you can mold your heart into one that is prepared to sacrifice so that you may live your dreams. It's daunting to stay focused when your environment is affluenza infected and ego based, in opposition to mastery. Because of this, you must constantly renew your mind, so that you can revisit your purpose and keep aware of your true self. Each day, the mind gets filled with needless debris, and so you must clear out what's not you

A Comparison of Mastery and Ego

Mastery	Ego
Strong sense of self	Self-conscious
Seeks the truth	Needs to be right
Self-confident	False bravado
Stable	Unpredictable
Self-education	Comparison with others
Win the battle within	Win at all costs
Process oriented	Outcome oriented
Best shot	Win or lose
Willing to look foolish	Afraid of humiliation
Fully present	Living in past and future
True to self	Unaware of true self
Willing to sacrifice	Seeks instant gratification
Ability to suffer/ be uncomfortable	Comfort seeking
Feeling of control	Controlled by results
Freedom and passion	Fear and tension
Embrace opponent	Hate/fear opponent
Humble	Arrogant
Seeks growth	Seeks validation
Big picture	Self-centered
Centered	Scattered
Seeks wisdom	Seeks status
Few needs	Needy
Purpose beyond goals	No real purpose
Unlimited imagination	Bounded by experience
Transcends circumstances	Attached to circumstances

and reboot the system (which you'll read about in Chapter 5).

The samurai spent much time in meditation, knowing that the slimmest mistake in moral judgment, which we take for granted today, would be fatal. If a samurai publicly disgraced another with harsh words, he might have been called upon to take his own life. Knowing this, the samurai had to keep their minds sharp, because their code demanded constant and severe accountability.

Renewing the mind starts with the awareness that human nature is self-centered and that every morning when we wake up, the mind leans in that direction. Because we are largely influenced by our feelings—be it hunger or anger or desire—we must learn to not get caught up in frustration with the past or anxiety about the future. With frustration and anxiety we become careless and less aware—of our goals, of the present moment, of opportunities.

> Your time is limited, so don't waste it living someone else's life. . . . have the courage to follow your heart and intuition. . . . Remembering that I'll be dead soon is the most important tool I've ever encountered to help me make the big choices in life. . . . All external expectations, all pride, all fear of embarrassment or failure—these things just fall away in the face of death, leaving only what is truly important.
>
> —**Steve Jobs, founder, Apple Computers, after being diagnosed with cancer**

One way to stay sharp is to remember that this moment is all we've got. Tomorrow may never come. It's commonplace to take for granted everything we have and expect to have those same things tomorrow. It's an attachment that limits us. One difference I've noticed in my travels to developing countries is that they have fewer attachments. They often are more joyful because they appreciate what they have. They also have a different attitude toward death. In Africa death is part of the circle of life, whereas in North America death is generally not to be discussed and a shock when it comes. If, counter to the norm, we can accept that we will die, perhaps much sooner than we wish, we can start living and get past our fears.

Recently I was speaking to a group of business executives who had flown in from around North America. I really wanted to speak well and began to feel attached to the outcome of my presentation and had the anxiousness that accompanies attachment. Not wanting that attachment, I thought about the samurai. I did some deep breathing to get centered and told myself, "The reality is, today could be your last day. You may not see tomorrow. Don't be so naive and careless to think that tomorrow is a certainty. Since that's the case, this may be your last talk." With those few moments of clearing my mind and having that little talk with myself, my preoccupation with myself faded as I focused on connecting with the audience and sharing from my heart.

The samurai rid themselves of everything that would divert their focus from what was most important. That cleansing allowed them to live fearlessly and take risks that derive from unrestricted freedom. Their code of honor superseded their very lives and thus prevented them from being swayed by fear or outside influences. Samurai were extremely self-disciplined and lived highly in the present by maintaining constant awareness of their own mortality.

Death is often linked with suffering. In Western culture, suffering is to be avoided at all costs. That posture of avoidance is detrimental, because, with obvious exceptions (such as abuse), those who want to learn self-mastery and live powerful lives would do better to embrace suffering rather than escape from it. Self-control and suffering are interwoven. Think of the people who have been most respected worldwide throughout history: Mahatma Gandhi, Nelson Mandela, Martin Luther King Jr., Mother Teresa—they all suffered and were prepared to suffer. Moreover, they all had strong character built out of this suffering. Without pain and affliction, there is no growth. If you think of the people you know or have met who have the most character and inner peace, it is doubtless that they have been tested. Winston Churchill summed it up when he said, "Those destined for greatness must first walk alone in the desert."

Sport psychologists Terry Orlick and Shauna Burke interviewed mountain climbers who successfully reached the summit of Mount Everest. When asked what it took to achieve that goal, one climber said:

> The greatest most single thing is to experience hardship. I have suffered a lot on other expeditions before going to Everest. People often ask me what it takes to do Everest and to be honest it is a lifetime of suffering. That is what you draw on, that ability to say I can sustain the suffering. Climbing Everest is like an aching tiredness that goes right into the depths of your soul. So the first time hardship shows up on Everest, and it is a very long suffering period, you are able to endure because you say, "Yes, I have suffered like this before and I have suffered for protracted periods of time."

Suffering gets our attention in a way that other experiences cannot. It is often the only thing that can break through our shell of self-centeredness, expanding our awareness, inviting compassion and connection with others. Then we can see further, from a new

Dostoevsky said, "There is only one thing that I dread: not to be worthy of my sufferings." These words frequently came to my mind after I became acquainted with those martyrs whose behavior in [concentration] camp, whose suffering and death bore witness to the fact that the last inner freedom cannot be lost. . . . They were worthy of their sufferings; the way they bore their suffering was a genuine inner achievement. It is this spiritual freedom—which cannot be taken away—that makes life meaningful and purposeful.

—Dr. Viktor Frankl, holocaust survivor and author, *Man's Search for Meaning*

angle, with more meaning and clarity. It may be only with eyes rinsed with tears that we can truly see who we are.

How did Nelson Mandela suffer through twenty-seven years of false imprisonment only to emerge without bitterness toward his captors and end centuries of apartheid? Daily suffering molded him. Who could have known what awaited Mandela—that he would become president, lead South Africa out of apartheid, and change the world—after imprisonment? Neither can you know the greatness to come *because* of *your* pain.

Madiba, as South Africans respectfully call Nelson Mandela, came to visit the South African Olympic Team in the Olympic Village prior to the start of the Sydney Olympics. His arrival caused quite a stir, and meeting him was an amazing honor. As he stood there giving a little talk and wishing us luck, I couldn't help but consider his unique sacrifice for his country and willingness to put his people's needs before his own. Mandela was willing to suffer, and through his suffering he became one of the world's most widely respected leaders.

Perhaps the biggest challenge with suffering is not the suffering itself, but the mind that is afraid of the suffering that may continue. Whether it's imprisonment, physical pain, or belt-tightening to survive tough financial times, you can usually handle it for a short period. It's the fear of having to endure hardship for an extended period that is the problem.

Most often, the biggest component in suffering is fear, a future-oriented line of thinking. What's going to happen to me? Or, when will it stop? Because of this, we want to run from it, but that's usually a mistake. Suffering produces perseverance, perseverance produces character, and character is the basis for the quiet inner confidence that becomes a powerful sense of self.

To embrace suffering is to silence the Critic, since to the ego and the Critic suffering is bad. This acceptance transcends our circumstances; we're no longer enslaved to what's happening, liberated from our mind and body and all the associated ups and downs. The truth is that our suffering need not be an obstacle to the joy and peace we desire. It can actually become the means to joy and peace.

We will suffer. Every moment of discomfort offers the chance to resist or embrace the suffering. When we resist hardship our perspective narrows. The suffering seems worse and we feel victimized. "Why is this happening to me?" we ask in self-pity. Learning and growth are impaired as fear moves in.

When we embrace hardship with the belief that we are never given more than we can handle, our perspective widens (see Figure 4.1). Knowing that we need adversity to grow, we look for the lesson. Often without suffering we would never stop to look. When we do we can learn and grow.

Love, wisdom, and courage enable us to grow from the suffering. Love focuses on the big picture, on others, which helps us get through the suffering. Wisdom sees the growth and freedom beyond

Figure 4.1 **The Lifeline of Suffering and Growth**

the suffering, and courage allows us to be present in the suffering to learn and grow.

The 12-Step Model

Another group of people who know suffering found a method to not only transcend their afflictions but also conquer their demons and change lives all over the world. During the economic depression of the 1930s, Bill Wilson became an alcoholic and was introduced to a powerful way of life that enabled him to overcome his addiction to alcohol. As cofounder of Alcoholics Anonymous (AA), Wilson, along with Dr. Bob Smith, built a 12-step program that has been adopted all over the world to surmount myriad addictions and sufferings.

The program addresses the three dimensions of the human experience: physical, mental, and spiritual. Physically, individuals cannot change under their own power. Mentally, they know that how they're living is hurting them, but that knowledge along with the desire to change is not enough. The root of the malady is spiritual.

The illness in all 12-step groups is considered to be self-centeredness. The process of working the steps is intended to replace self-centeredness with a growing moral consciousness and a willingness to engage in self-sacrifice and unselfish constructive action. The twelve steps help the members overcome their self-centeredness through the following principles:

+ A willingness to die to their old nature and its way of doing things
+ A search for self-awareness to see things as they really are
+ A vision beyond themselves to connect with a higher power and others

Service to Others

These same principles have worked in 12-step programs all around the world—in Japan with the samurai, as well as with elite athletes. New York Giants football star David Tyree knows about dying to self. As a pro football player, Tyree went down a road of self-centered behavior that led to drug use and then jail time. One day things changed. The wide receiver known for his miraculous catch in the 2008 Super Bowl said the turning point for him was to accept "a certain level of surrender" to forces stronger than football or its players. "Surrender is not a popular term when you're talking amongst men," he said, "but, honestly, that's really what it takes."

When you see how a powerful team sacrifices the needs of the individual for the overall good, and how this approach helps each team member, then the value of sacrificing yourself (and the self-centeredness that leads toward fear) becomes more apparent. As described in Chapter 3, Lewis Pugh overcame his fears and doubts through a powerful connection to others and a purpose beyond himself. He was thereby able to face his own possible death with confidence and aggression. The samurai lived in service to others with a selflessness that took precedence over their own lives; they were even willing to die for these ideals. AA members have a covenant based on dying to their old selves, humility, service, and connection to others.

The Eight Attachments

The main challenge we face in the pursuit of mastery is our self-centeredness, and one of the most blatant ways self-centeredness limits us is through our attachments. As we go through life, we develop habits of thinking and feeling—patterns that direct our lives. Some of those patterns, perhaps subconsciously, slowly transform our hearts—and the desires that go along with the heart—into attachments.

For example, by this stage in your life you've probably developed some sort of reputation. Perhaps you've worked extremely hard and are known as a dedicated worker, a loyal friend, or a trusted leader. Through these years of hard work, you've built an image, and when you work very hard for something, you can easily become attached to it and may even feel entitled to it. Maybe you "deserve" it.

Or perhaps you're an Olympic swimmer. Imagine you swim the 100-meter butterfly, and you've proved you are the best butterfly swimmer in the country. You've trained every day for four years, and now the time has come for your event, which lasts one minute. You could easily become attached to the outcome of the event. It may not even be a sporting event: it could be your job, your house, or anything else.

The problem is that you cannot fully control what people think of you, nor whether you win an event, keep a job, or even live to see tomorrow, and when you're attached to something that you can't fully control, you live under the constant threat of losing it. If, however, you can give up your attachment to what you cannot control—even if it's one of the most important things in your life—then you can have the inner peace and presence that allow you to perform your best and live with freedom and passion. You can be fearless.

In 2007 the University of British Columbia (UBC) men's golf team, pursuing a national championship, fell apart amid high expectations. During the four-day tournament, they desperately wanted to win but were unable to enjoy the game or stay present, and as the rounds progressed, they became more nervous and self-conscious. They lost. The year 2008 was a different story as they began to work with the author. They became the first foreign team in history to win the National Association of Intercollegiate Athletics (NAIA) national championship, and they followed up a few weeks later by winning the Canadian national championship. Team captain Sean Hurley explains what changed: "In '07 we were a bunch of individuals trying so hard to meet expectations and win. Everything changed in '08. Working with Jim, winning was not a 'materiality' to us anymore. We focused on playing with passion with and for each other and let the chips fall where they may. Our mantra was, 'The score is for the fans—we play for the love of the game.'"

To gain maximum freedom, you must be willing to fail and not be attached to your desires. With no expectations of how things need to unfold, you're free to handle any obstacle. In the pursuit of mastery, these eight attachments, in no particular order, affect you the most:

1. How others see you

2. Your money and possessions

3. What you want (goals)

4. Comfort

5. Your past

6. How things are (status quo)

7. Expectations

8. Your self

The key is to live as if you'll die tomorrow and prepare as if you'll live forever. That said, how do we rid ourselves of these attachments and obsessions? Or you could say, how do we achieve self-mastery, since self-mastery is largely a matter of dropping your attachments. Here are a few ways:

Remember that you may not live to see tomorrow. Develop more gratitude. Focus on self-awareness and personal growth. Pursue a purpose beyond yourself. Serve others.

These five methods are not necessarily foolproof, but if you adopt them in your thoughts and pursuits, your life will change. A purpose beyond yourself will emerge with more clarity as you serve, and you'll connect with others more powerfully and gain a foundation that will set your course in the right direction. Your joy will increase through the joy of others. Pulitzer Prize nominee Frederick Buechner said, "Vocation comes from the place of intersect where the world's great need meets our deep gladness."

As we develop self-awareness and uncover our gifts, we are better able to see the match between our place in the world and our higher purpose. The journey of self-awareness and higher purpose is the path toward freedom.

In your quest for success, the ultimate triumph is to be your true self—the best part of you, fearless and fully present, constantly seeking to learn and grow and to help others do the same. To do this, you must be willing to die, by way of sacrificing your old, self-centered nature and putting your ego aside for something greater. It's hard, because you'll have to face your fears. You will suffer, but in embracing the suffering, you'll gain discipline, and with discipline comes honor. If there is something that is so valuable and meaningful that you would sacrifice your life for it, then you have found a way to be fearless.

To live fearlessly is to live a life of freedom, one uninhibited by societal restraint, one of taking risks, of going to the edge and looking over the cliff simply for the more expansive view, without trembling or hesitation. It's not for everyone. In fact, it's not for most. It's a challenge for the courageous.

What I'm asking you to do is to put your *self* on the line, heart and soul, to test who you are. I want you to see if you're being true to yourself or are instead filled with attachments to external things and the self-consciousness that comes with trying to please others and fit in. In preparing for today as if it were your last day alive, you are choosing a life filled with growth and sacred moments.

Key Points from Chapter 4

- Extraordinary success is the by-product of self-mastery.
- Self-consciousness and attachment are two of the biggest obstacles to extraordinary success. The ego amplifies those obstacles, and mastery diminishes them.
- Mastery is made of self-awareness, self-discipline, and personal growth.
- Embrace suffering, and the real possibility of death, in order to grow toward Zoë.
- The ego is caught up in temporary pleasure, while mastery is focused on permanent and powerful virtues.

Follow-Up Questions and Activities

- What are *your* attachments?
- What are you holding on to so tightly that it affects your relationships, growth, or performance?
- How does self-consciousness affect you? In which roles or life situations do you compare yourself with others?

- Use your journal to record your attachments and how you can pursue your goals without letting doubts, fears, and neediness stall your growth.
- Each day when you wake up, ask yourself how you would live if this were your last day.
- How can you orient your environment around self-mastery? What limits your pursuit of mastery?

Change Your State, Change Your Life

How to Get the Feelings You Want

It is the mark of an educated man to be able to entertain a thought without accepting it.

—**Aristotle**

Change or die: what if you were given that choice? Could you change your life if you really had to? Most people who have successfully made important changes in their lives did so by learning to influence their emotions, according to Alan Deutschman, an author of several books on change and innovation. You may realize that you need to think more positively or exercise more often but find yourself struggling to turn those realizations into habits. Obstacles arise and bring you down emotionally, and so you regroup until something sparks your resurgence. In order to be true to yourself and live courageously, you must be able to change.

If you want to make positive changes that last and to continually expand what you believe is possible, you must learn to direct how you feel.

Feelings run our lives. When we feel good, we take setbacks in stride, see more opportunities, and find beauty to be just a little more apparent. When we feel bad, obstacles become larger and more difficult to overcome. Life becomes a constant reaction to circumstances and to the thoughts and feelings that result. We become pawns of the environment, bumped from circumstance to circumstance. In the negative environment in which we live, this condition is problematic. If we stay in a constant state of reaction, we have little control and persistently feel negative. Those repeated feelings become patterns, and the patterns become beliefs.

> We don't have power because we are constantly reacting to the outer world. You are either consciously creating your life or you are reacting to it.
>
> —John Kehoe,
> *Mind Power into the Twenty-First Century*

Beliefs are habits of behavior and expectation that are formed, as we will discuss in Chapter 6, from how we interpret the events in our lives. (Feelings and beliefs are largely intertwined and so Chapters 5 and 6 will be also.) We each have our own filter that determines how we see the world, and that filter creates the meaning that defines our experience. So, in this chapter we'll learn to create the feelings we want, more often, which will pave the way for empowering beliefs. We'll look at how to manage our state by examining three areas that profoundly affect it: our attention, our desires, and our physiology. We will address how to maximize emotional control and minimize the limitations of fear, doubt, and frustration.

A Few Words on Feelings

We defined Zoë in Chapter 3 as absolute fullness of life. It comes from a state of resonance, in which we feel connected and congruent, fully engaged in what we love. While Zoë goes far beyond feelings, we recognize it by the feel of it. In our discussion, our *state* and our *feelings* are used interchangeably. Our emotions and desires are part of our state.

Psychologist Robert Vallerand identified seven basic emotions: happiness, interest, surprise, fear, anger, guilt, and sadness. Every other emotion essentially is a derivative of those seven. Each of the seven basic emotions is useful in one way or another, and with the exception of guilt and sadness, they all provide energy (though the energy from fear may propel us or stop us). Anger is an interesting emotion because it produces a lot of energy and has the potential to strongly affect performance. For most of us, anger is a response to frustration that decreases our ability to focus and make quality decisions. We should be aware of how it affects us and our performance. Anger, as is true of frustration and fear, is usually a symptom of a self-occupied mind that is not seeing the bigger picture.

Feelings include the sensations we have in the body that come directly from our five senses. When we feel the water hitting us in the face as we dive into the pool, the skis hitting the snow, or the bat hitting the ball, we notice the event through our senses. We experience the world through our senses and through the imagination. When what we physically touch, smell, taste, hear, and see enters the mind, we do some internal computations to decide the meaning and then react or respond in some fashion.

In the next chapter we'll discuss those computations and perceptions that lead to beliefs. Here we will look at setting up favorable conditions for those computations. That is, we will learn how to create more positive feelings that will help us perceive the events in our lives with far greater vision. In a positive frame of mind, we can bring our best selves to the situations we encounter.

Our thoughts affect how we feel, and how we feel affects how we think. Our thoughts and feelings trigger chemical and electrical reactions in the brain that can be powerful enough to speed healing or cause ulcers, or, on a day-to-day basis, free us from tension or fill us with anxiety. Our thoughts show up in the body as feelings, sickness, health, confidence, and so on. How we carry ourselves on the outside—what we do with our bodies—affects how we feel on the inside. If we want change—and all of us who are goal oriented (or dream oriented) want change—then we must work from the outside in as well as from the inside out.

What Gets Your Attention Gets You

If there is one powerful thing that self-actualizing people have learned to do, it's to control where they place their attention. They have built their environment, formed relationships, and focused their desires around that which inspires, teaches, and empowers. Author Dr. E. Stanley Jones, a friend of Gandhi's, said it well: "What gets your attention gets *you*." It *gets* you. Your thoughts become feelings, moods, and attitudes that direct your life. They become you.

Think of how your state is affected when you're watching a movie. If the movie is engaging, your whole being is caught up in it. Your heart rate speeds up as if you're the one being chased, or you'll start to cry as if you're the one with the broken heart. Your mind, unable to differentiate between reality and what you vividly imagine, feels it as real. Movies are so powerful because they greatly influence your state.

When you realize how sensitive you truly are to sensory input and to what degree it affects your state, you begin to understand that every image has a consequence. Every image that enters your mind produces a thought. Thoughts

> The proper emotional response to a problem is 75 percent of the solution.
>
> —Jim Loehr, Ph.D.,
> *Mental Toughness*
> *Training for Sports*

are powerful forces. Your life unfolds the way it does because of your thoughts. To change your behavior, you need to change your thoughts, and to change your thoughts, you must change where you focus your attention.

Objects that come through your field of vision affect you immensely. Whether it's a beautiful sunset, a masterful piece of art, or a stunning photograph, they all provoke feelings. To have good feelings more often, you need more good images consistently running through your mind. They can take the form of words, symbols, songs, or pictures. Of course, you can combine them too: a collage with pictures of your goals along with positive words is powerful. You can use those words to make affirmations (see Chapter 6), or add pictures and a soundtrack to make a movie. (Go to innerexcellence.com for helpful tips.) When you realize how much the words and images in your mind affect your life, you'll take more care to make sure the words and images are positive ones.

The Power of Desire and Honor

How we feel is largely impacted by how we direct our desires. Desires influence our perception, what we strive for, and where our heart goes. One reason the affluenza virus is so perilous is that it creates a continuous craving for more awards, more stuff, and more status that is never filled. When we do not get what we desire, frustration sets in as expectations go unmet. The solution is not to abandon our desires, but to make sure our desires are taking us where we really want to go. Our hearts get molded around that which we desire. Who we become is largely a function of how we direct our desires.

Desires out of control create addictions and obsessions that cause us to lose out on the joy and passion of performance and life. When we're hungry, we must eat; when we want chocolate, we must have it. Desires are very powerful, but they can turn on us. Our human nature will always lead us to seek immediate gratification. Discipline is the ability to delay gratification, to reject some desires and accept others. Desire is a marvelous motivator and terrible master. If we were to continually give in to all of our desires, we'd overeat, oversleep, and max out our credit cards. We'd become slaves to our desires.

Desires lead to feelings, and feelings generally win out over willpower. In other words, we may know what we should do, but we don't do it. Our feelings control us. However, it does not have to be this way. Dr. Dallas Willard, former director of the USC School of Philosophy, says, "Those dominated by the ego believe their feelings must be satisfied." When you let go of your ego and gain self-mastery, you'll no longer be a slave to your feelings. You can develop more self-control and learn to reject the desires that are not empowering before they become too much to handle.

We've all been able to reject some desires because they were out of the question in relation to our values. You may desperately want something but will not steal to get it. The problem comes when we continually give in to our desires such that we can no longer reject the ones we used to, because we let our desires get out of hand.

Take eating, for example. The more you give in to eating things you normally wouldn't, the easier it is to give in. Consider if you were to purposely go without food for a period of time (after consulting your doctor). At a basic level, fasting is the rejection of desires and overcoming of feelings. Once you've gone a day or two without food, you gain a sense of power because you are no longer a slave to your cravings for food. You don't "have to" eat. When "have to" feelings constantly drive your behavior, you open yourself up to frustration and anxiety because you don't always get what you "have to" get. What you need is access to more "want to" feelings.

Just as eating healthily creates a desire for more healthful food, and exercising creates a desire for regular exercise, we can increase our desire for empowering habits. When you connect with your true self and focus on that which builds the mind, body, and spirit, you increase your ability to reject unhealthful desires. Within you is a deep desire for honor and integrity. Increasing the levels of honor and integrity increases self-acceptance. One of the most powerful ways of doing this is to have a purpose beyond yourself. If the purpose of your life is based on something beyond your own needs and wants, you'll be better able to reject the desires that are not taking you where you ultimately want to go.

Controlling Your Physiology

As you focus your attention and desires on that which empowers, you will notice a major impact on how you feel each day. Another important issue is not just where you focus your attention, but how. How do you learn to focus your attention in a world with ever-increasing demands on your time and energy?

Three major factors affect your attention: the quality of your nutrition, the quality and intensity of your exercise, and the percentage of your time spent on attention-deficit activities versus attention-building activities. Watching television and surfing the Internet, as mentioned in Chapter 1, are two of today's prime attention-deficit activities. Video games seem to have a similar effect. Attention-improving activities are ones that clear the mind and challenge it. Practicing yoga, meditating, keeping a journal, running, playing chess, and doing crossword puzzles are a few examples. Having quiet time is a prerequisite to improving focus. Of course, simply practicing paying attention is also important; you'll learn how to be more present in Chapter 7.

Your ability to pay attention and be present is largely affected by your physiology. There's a lot more to it than just exercise and nutrition. Your posture, your muscle tension, how you breathe, how much sleep you get, whether your eyes are focused above or below the horizon, and similar factors all have an impact on how you feel. (Note: placing your sight above the horizon, versus below, leads to better feelings—the old adage about keeping your chin up is valid.)

One important aspect of controlling your physiology, as well as your energy, is to walk with a swagger. How you carry yourself has a significant effect on how you feel inside. Walk with your head down and shoulders slumped—as we've all done after a mistake or setback—and your energy will drop. Walk with your head up and shoulders back, eyes above the horizon, and your feelings will be more positive.

In order to control your energy, you must train your mind, body, and spirit the way an athlete trains. Periods of intense activity should be followed by periods of rest and relaxation. You must take time to unplug the mind if you want to control your physiology. At the very least, you need to learn how to reboot the system.

One of the fundamental exercises in controlling your energy is to get centered. Getting centered is literally bringing your energy to the center of your body, just below your belly button. This is done by controlling the flow of oxygen and focusing your mind on that activity. The idea is to shut down the mind in order to recharge.

Here's an exercise that you should become proficient at performing, so try it now. First, find a good posture, ideally sitting up straight. Generally, it's easier if you close your eyes. Take a long, slow, deep breath in through your nose, expanding your ribs, allowing the air to fill your stomach. Hold it for a few seconds, and then slowly exhale through your nose or mouth, deflating your stomach, allowing your belly button to approach your spine. Hold your breath for a few seconds before you inhale again. As you do this, note any tension in the facial muscles, and let them relax. Allow your jaw to hang. These are both crucial elements, as tension is often stored in the jaw and in the muscles around it (a helpful point to remember in pressure situations).

Deep breathing should be done anytime you're anxious or nervous, when your heart is beating fast or your mind is racing. To slow down your heart rate or racing mind, slow down your breathing. Building on this basic exercise, we now add a few variations. The first one is to imagine that with every breath in, you're inhaling life-giving energy, and with every breath out, all your cares, concerns, or worries are leaving your body. (You can also visualize the life-giving energy entering your body as a mist to enhance the picture.) Next we add positive thoughts to the breathing. In his book, *Coaching the Artist Within*, Dr. Eric Maisel has provided a powerful exercise he calls the centering sequence that begins with "I am completely stopping." Try this now: To turn off your mind, you will say, "I am . . . " in your mind as you breathe in, and "completely stopping" as you breathe out. If you want, you can imagine yourself descending a staircase, slowly going down to a quiet, peaceful place. You're shutting down the system.

There are a number of variations to try next. In place of "I am . . . completely stopping," you can use any of these variations:

- I am . . . fully present.
- I am . . . confident and focused.
- I am . . . calm and relaxed.
- I am . . . letting go.
- I am . . . brilliant and successful.
- I am . . . an all-star.
- I am . . . [add however you want to feel or be].
- Focus . . . and enjoy.
- Relax . . . and smile.

◈ "I Expect . . . Nothing"

There is a samurai saying: "Expect nothing, prepare for anything." Expectations are a potentially large stumbling block in performance, causing tension and fear, taking you out of the present. By definition, expectation implies looking to the future. Centering exercises are done to bring your energy to your body's center and your mind to the present. "I expect . . . nothing" is a powerful centering exercise that says you have no needs; you can handle any circumstance. You have no expectations about how things *should* be.

Imagine a samurai before a sword fight in which one person will die. To be his best, the samurai must stay focused and centered the entire time. He especially cannot afford to be flustered by unforeseen circumstances. Expectation, as we use the word, has nothing to do with confidence, which is faith in the future. It is simply anticipation of future circumstances, which we want to avoid. We prepare for the future every day by goal setting, affirmations, and visualizing future outcomes. Otherwise, we want to stay fully in the present.

The ego, the Trickster, the Critic, and the Monkey Mind all continuously try to take us to the past and future, which is much of their strength. Learning to expect nothing and be prepared for anything is a good way to stay present and win the inner battle.

Say, for example, you're driving to an important meeting. You start to get nervous. Your mind begins to race, and your heart rate speeds up. You pull over. You know this is not how you want to feel, so you decide to get centered. You take three or four long, slow, deep breaths and then say, "I expect . . . nothing." Your racing mind begins to settle down, and in just a few minutes your heart rate has returned to normal. You feel better—still nervous perhaps, but not so scattered.

Expectations are often the toughest when you've done something in the past (won a championship or landed a major account, for example) and feel you're expected to do it again. Perhaps your past performance resulted in the signing of a big contract or a promotion, and everyone has been saying how great you'll be. Now everything you do, large or small, comes with others constantly expecting the same success. It's easy to get overwhelmed. Sometimes in golf the five-foot putt is a lot harder than the ten-foot putt, all because of expectations.

A Few More Variations on Centering

Another option in centering is to repeat the preceding exercise but slowly eliminate words until only one word remains. Let's use "Be here . . . right now" as an example. On your first breath, you say, "Be here" on the inhale and "right now" on the exhale. On your second breath, you say, "Be here" on the inhale and "now" on the exhale. On the third breath, you say, "Be" on the inhale and "here" on the exhale. On the forth breath, you say, "Be" on the inhale and nothing on the exhale.

Yet another useful centering exercise, for those who believe in a Higher Power, goes like this: "Be still and know . . . that I am God." That's your first complete breath. On your second breath, you say, "Be still and know . . . that I am." The third breath is, "Be still . . . and know." The fourth breath is, "Be . . . still." The last breath is, "Be."

Centering exercises are to be used throughout the day, every day, not just when you think you need to be at your best. If you want to have a clear mind when you perform, you need to practice getting centered daily so that you can do it under pressure when you need it most.

Another variation with getting centered is to add an image that represents how you want to feel. It may be a picture in your mind of one of your best performances, or it may be an image of your next performance.

Erica K., a dancer with the Mexican national ballet team, would go out onto the stage hours before anyone arrived and stand quietly at center stage. She would take some deep breaths and imagine reaching out to the entire crowd and giving them a group hug before a big performance. Then she'd imagine energy coming from above, flowing through her to everyone in attendance. She'd become one with the audience and everything in the environment. Erica imagined perfect harmony and generated powerful feelings as part of her preperformance routine. This allowed her to perform with confidence and grace.

Anchoring and Releasing Different States

One of the challenges associated with emotions such as frustration, sadness, or fear is that we don't see possibilities. In those instances you need more options. One powerful way of gaining more options is to be able to either latch onto or release a feeling, depending on whether it serves you well. If you're frustrated, angry, or anxious, you can often turn that around, sometimes in an instant. That feeling can almost always be countered successfully by changing perspective in order to change your perception of the event. Change what you see, hear, and feel, and your feelings will change.

Before key moments you must know how you want to feel and how to get that feeling when you want it. For example, you've likely had amazing performances in which everything felt right and you were totally caught up in the moment. That's how you want to feel each time you perform. If you were to imagine that exact situation again and recall every sight, smell, sound, taste, and feel of the moment, you would be able to feel what you felt as if it were happening again. You want to be able to regularly access that feeling, to have it on speed dial. One way to do that is by creating an anchor.

An anchor is a sight, sound, taste, feel, or smell that is linked to a feeling. Anchors are created all the time in your life without your knowing it. For example, when a song comes on from your senior year in high school, usually it evokes memories that may have strong feelings attached to them. Music is an anchor that can powerfully trigger a feeling.

To anchor a specific feeling, introduce a stimulus that you repeat to associate it with that feeling. Ivan Pavlov, for example, anchored his dogs by ringing a bell before he fed them, so that eventually just ringing the bell caused the dogs to salivate. You can anchor the feeling you want by ringing a bell, smelling a scent, clenching your fist, clapping your hands, or doing anything else each time you get that feeling.

For example, think of a moment when you felt incredibly confident and powerful. The more details you remember, the stronger the feeling gets. If you want to anchor that feeling, when the feeling hits its highest point, or just before, smell something strong and soothing, such as peppermint oil. Practice visualizing that moment, get the feeling, and then smell the peppermint. This process creates an anchor to peppermint and helps you bring back that feeling in the future when you may need it most. The next time you want confidence, smell the peppermint.

While we all have our unique primary sensory modes of remembering and experiencing events, smell is usually the strongest anchor of any sense. Smell seems to have a direct pipeline to feelings.

There are times, of course, when we're in an unresourceful state and we want to change how we feel. To release an unwanted emotion, we can learn to disassociate from it. It's not repressing the feelings; it's learning to change them to better ones. When we repress feelings, we become numb, but when we learn to control and direct our feelings, we become powerful. Just as we learned to anchor good emotions and reexperience them, we also must learn to manage negative feelings.

One way to remove the negative feelings from a situation is to see yourself literally far away from the experience or emotion that you don't want. Say, for example, you're anxious about an upcoming performance. You can disassociate from the anxiety by visualizing yourself floating up and away from it all. Try this exercise for disassociation:

1. Sit in a chair and get centered. Become aware of your body. Sense your body's weight on the chair and any other feelings in your body. Often when people feel good, they feel it in the chest, and when they feel not so good, they feel it in the stomach.

2. Imagine floating out of your body to the ceiling. See yourself and the room below in precise detail.

3. Float above the room and over the building so that you can see the surrounding area. Continue to float up, and see the entire city as well as any rivers or other landmarks. See the mountains if there are any. Continue up through the clouds so high that you can see all the neighboring cities and mountain ranges and neighboring states. Continue up higher and see the entire state or province, and then still higher and see the entire continent and now the oceans and all the continents as you see the spherical earth. While you're rising, check back in every now and then and remember where you are below: see the building, and then see the surrounding area, the city, the state, and

so on. As you get higher and higher, feel how free and peaceful it is as you soar. When you're ready, begin descending. As you get closer to your chair, feel all your cares and concerns leaving as you drop down to Earth.

Another way to disassociate from an unwanted feeling or state is to reframe how you see the situation. That is, see the situation from another vantage point, in a different context, or even as if you were observing yourself. Here is a powerful exercise developed by NLP creators Richard Bandler and John Grinder that reduces unwanted fears and feelings from any memory. It could be anything you want to change how you feel about, from the fear of public speaking to a golfer's fear of hitting the ball into the hazard.

Imagine you are alone, sitting in a movie theater, about to watch yourself on the screen. Actually you'll be watching whatever stressful event provoked or is provoking the anxiety in your life. (You're going to revisit the most dramatic/difficult memory of whatever it is that you're fearful or anxious about.) Now float up into the projection booth and see yourself at the controls of the projector. See yourself watching yourself through the glass, in your seat, watching yourself up on the screen.

Turn the projector on, and run the movie of the stressful event, in black and white, from before the event happened until the event is totally over and everything is OK. (Because you're "disassociated" from the event by watching yourself watching yourself, you'll feel less tension than you normally would.) Pause the movie at the end and float down into the theater and then go into the movie, so you're actually back at the fearful or anxious event, just after it finished.

Now rewind, in full color with sound, the whole movie in about two seconds, all the way back until before the event started. Now replay the event how you wanted it to go. Repeat this new, good movie, in full color, eight to twelve times.

What happens is that your mind had a clear picture and program for that trigger (public speaking audiences, water hazards on the golf course, spiders, etc.) and now you've blurred the memory. Done correctly, the fear goes away. When you learn to manipulate the images in your mind by altering the variables that affect that image (context, sound, light, smell, etc.) you can anchor or release whatever images and feelings you want.

 ## Memories Versus Current Feelings

As I just mentioned, certain anchors will trigger unwanted memories. They may be tied to feelings that are not relevant or useful to how we feel today. For example, when you hear a song on the radio that reminds you of a past relationship, you may miss that person and feel sad, even if you are currently doing well, are in a good relationship, and are happy. When you realize that it's just a memory of how you previously felt and not how you feel today, you can dismiss the feeling much more readily.

Consider an example in which you performed poorly at a certain venue. Even if it's been several years since you've performed there, the next time you're scheduled to appear, the Trickster will remind you of your poor performance, and you may be beaten even before you get there. The subconscious reviews every situation in life and pulls up any emotional events tied to the current situation so that it can place it in context. The Trickster, however, always remembers past failures of similar events and projects them to the future, even if you're much better at what you do now.

As you develop your ability to direct your emotions, you'll increase your awareness of your feelings and be able to sense their origins and deal with them in increasingly better ways. If you're feeling down and you realize that some trigger reminded you of a past failure, you can remind yourself that you are a much different person from the one you were back then. If you're frustrated because things aren't going your way, you can get centered and then be able to release that feeling with the reframing/disassociation exercise. In the next chapter we'll look at how to control our perceptions in order to create the meanings that lead to powerful beliefs.

Key Points from Chapter 5

- Freedom comes from having the courage to change; to change our lives, we must learn how to change our state.
- Your state is the combination of the pictures in your mind, your physiology, and your desires.
- How we direct our desires largely affects our ability to control our feelings.
- We must focus our attention on that which empowers and learn how to control our attention (with nutrition, exercise, and attention-building activities).
- Getting centered is a way of controlling the flow of oxygen and your thoughts to bring your energy to the body's center.
- Expectations of how things should be is a future orientation, taking us out of the present, inviting doubts and fears.
- We can anchor the feelings we want and change to a more resourceful state when we're not feeling how we want to feel.

Follow-Up Questions and Activities

- Take an inventory of past performances, good and bad, and look for patterns in the emotions you felt. How do emotions affect your performance? How did those emotions come about?
- Think of your environment at home and at work. What are the images, words, and sounds in that environment? What can you do to put more empowering images and words into that space?
- Commit to getting centered twice a day this week for three minutes each time. Do it when you're frustrated, upset, nervous, angry, or anytime you're not present. Record in your journal how it affected you.
- How much time do you spend on attention-deficit activities versus attention-building activities? What do you need to sacrifice to balance the scales?
- Consider making a collage of your goals and dreams, or even a movie. Start collecting photographs and ideas of who you want to be, how you want to live, and exactly what you want in your life.
- Take an inventory of your greatest fear or anxiety producing memory. Go through the reframing exercise and see how that changes the memory.

The World Is Flat

*Reconstruct Your Model
of the World*

In the sky, there is no distinction between east and west; people create distinctions in their own minds and then believe them to be true.

—**Gautama Siddhartha, Zen master**

Tyrone ran for the fence but didn't quite make it. The store owner unloaded his shotgun at the kids who he thought broke his window. Little Ty got hit multiple times. He was five years old. He grew up in the Lafayette Court Housing Project of East Baltimore. His father was a drug dealer and spent most of Ty's childhood in prison. It was a time of survival. Tyrone saw a kid get stabbed multiple times, another beaten to death with a baseball bat, and another shot in the back on the basketball court. When asked about his childhood, he said, "It wasn't an easy life, but *it was the best for me.*" Five-feet-three-inch Tyrone "Muggsy"

Bogues went on to play fourteen years in the NBA, with metal slugs still embedded in his body from that day in East Baltimore.

Faced with overwhelming adversity, Muggsy found his way from the projects to playing in the NBA, from getting shot as a kid to shooting baskets for a living—a five-foot-three-inch miracle. He had talent—his forty-four-inch vertical jump attests to that—but he leveraged every inch with his mind. The five-year-old boy who got shot was overshadowed by the kid with a dream, one that he kept alive throughout his childhood. Muggsy had to use his imagination every day to feed this dream and develop the story that would one day unfold, as impossible as it was, just as he had imagined.

Everyone has a story. You are the author and narrator of your story; you choose which moments of life have meaning and how meaningful they are. Every moment provides you with an opportunity to decide in which direction your story will head. Every thought is part of the story line—great lives have great story lines. It's these thoughts, and how they get directed, that determine the course of your life. The pictures in your mind and the meaning you attach to them lay out the story. It's all too easy to forget your own story, the amazing one that waits to be written, as your imagination gets toned down by setbacks, logic, and rationalization. Of course it's ridiculous to think that a five-foot-three-inch kid from the ghetto can play in the NBA, but anything is possible in the imagination. If Muggsy can dream his life and live his dream, you can too.

By now we've worked through a few ideas on performance and freedom and how to combine the two. We live in a negative culture, one that lures us to find identity in external things, not our true selves. What's more, we each have a self-occupied nature that easily gets caught up in all our limitations and self-defeating thoughts. Thus, we miss out on opportunities to connect with beauty, with others, and with the bigger picture. So, we must learn how to abandon self-centeredness to gain the freedom to truly live.

In the previous chapter we learned how to control our state. Now we will search for the wisdom needed to see the world the way it really is, or at least closer to it, and the imagination to expand our vision and see more options. We will discuss how the way we process and give meaning to events creates our experience—and our experience is what matters. We will investigate how beliefs are formed and how to analyze and expand them.

 ## The Nature of Beliefs

Just as your perceptions are not actual reality, neither are beliefs. Beliefs are simply a programmed way of thinking that directs your behavior. It doesn't matter what so-called reality is; what matters is what you believe. Having the ability to win a match or execute a task makes no difference if you don't believe you can do it. Beliefs are programmed expectations that cause you to see what you expect to see and to achieve what you expect to achieve.

To children, the world is expansive and, more important, unlimited. As you grow up, that perspective changes. You have experiences that form your beliefs regarding what you can and can't do. You touch a hot stove and learn you can't do that without pain. Many of your experiences "teach" you what you can't do. Your efforts get dashed; your beliefs get challenged. Perhaps you liked to sing as a kid, and the first time you sang in front of others, people made fun of you. That early experience taught you that maybe you're not meant to be a singer or you're not very talented. You "learned" in that moment and created a belief about your singing. That belief may stay with you the rest of your life. What happened was that you had an experience that caused you to feel a certain way—in this case, rejected—and that occurrence set the bar for your beliefs about that area of your life. Unfortunately, most people simply give up on that skill or area of life, never finding out how good they could be if they challenged their limiting belief.

A belief can be created quickly—sometimes in only an instant—and then it stays with you, perhaps for a lifetime. Say, for example, you're an eight-year-old kid, and you see a dark, round shape as you climb into bed. Thinking it's a big spider, you scream, only to realize that it's not real: it's just a ball of yarn. The reality part doesn't matter. What matters is what you believe, and in that instant your brain believed it was a big spider. Also in that moment there was an emotional reaction of fear that your brain filed away, in order to protect you in the future. Your brain does its job, for the rest of your life, latching onto that fear whenever you see a spider or something that looks like one.

Thankfully, it doesn't have to be that way. If that fear of spiders, or any other belief, is not serving you how you'd like, you can change it. It doesn't matter how logical, ingrained, or traumatic your experience was that created that belief: you can unlearn what you learned. (The reframing exercise from Chapter 5 is one way.)

When you set a goal, examine what your beliefs are about that goal. You may ask yourself directly, "What are the three main beliefs I have around achieving this goal?" Is each belief useful for you now, in this situation? What would you have to believe to achieve your goal?

In the case of the fear of spiders, meaning was assigned into the arachnophobe's brain at the time of the incident. The same thing happens in other areas of life. With each new experience, your brain will attempt to assign meaning to the experience in order to understand how to respond. The brain goes through its checklist of questions: Is this relevant to me? What do I have in my databank of experiences that relates to this? Is this something I should be afraid of, or is it something I've mastered?

Beliefs not only set limits for what's possible in your life but also attract situations to try to keep those beliefs intact. It's called homeostasis. Homeostasis is the effort of the subconscious mind to maintain a certain level of skill or achievement, whatever the individual believes is right for him or her. For example, if you are performing above what you believe you are capable of doing, your subconscious will try to bring the performance down to your comfort level. By the same token, if you are performing below your level of belief, your subconscious will work to bring the results back up to your beliefs. It doesn't matter what you believe; your subconscious does not judge your belief. It tries only to make your beliefs happen. That's why beliefs are much more important than hopes and wishes. *You will always draw experiences into your life to support your beliefs.*

Your experiences create your beliefs, and your beliefs bring more of those experiences. If, for example, you have a favorable experience with a group of colleagues, then you become more comfortable around them, and your belief regarding your acceptance creates more favorable experiences. Of course, it goes the other way too. The important lesson is that you can control how you experience events, which affects your beliefs.

The Structure of Experience

The way we experience events seems pretty cut-and-dried: something happens, and we respond to it one way or another. If it's a good thing, we're happy; if it's a bad thing, we're upset. While this simple formula reflects how most of us experience the world, it's not the same for self-actualizers, who have in place a more developed mechanism to stand between the circumstances in their lives and how they respond.

We've all established patterns that determine whether we put the adversity in our lives to use or get pulled into despondency. It is our perception of an event and what we believe about it that determine how we experience the event—not the event itself. The fact that we want to get a promotion, score thirty points, or hit our quota is inconsequential compared with the belief we have about that goal and how we perceive our circumstances to be unfolding. Our cumulative perceptions about our experiences, what they mean and what we've learned, create the beliefs that allow us to overcome seemingly impossible odds. Of course, they also create the limits that restrict lives. Perception is all-important.

We experience the world in two primary ways: through the five senses of sight, sound, taste, smell, and feel, and with the imagination. Something enters our perception, and the nervous system notifies the brain of the stimulus. Alternatively, we place a picture in our minds through the imagination, and since the brain cannot tell the difference between what is vividly imagined and what is real, it processes the imagined stimulus in the same manner. There need not be an activating event.

Let's say I invite you into my kitchen, and we walk over to my cutting board. I have a bag of big, juicy lemons, and I cut one in half. Now I'm going to ask you to tilt your head back, open your mouth, and close your eyes for a few seconds. What happens next? Imagine the lemon half being held over your mouth and a hint of citrus in the air. A drop of juice hits your tongue. If you vividly followed along, you undoubtedly started to salivate. Your imagination can create reality—anytime, anywhere.

Since so many stimuli permeate the environment at any one time, we learn to filter our senses, consciously and unconsciously. We delete, distort, and generalize in order to make sense of things and not get overwhelmed. As we encounter the world, the information gets sorted in reference to our individual identity and beliefs in order to establish relevance and level of importance. Meaning is applied, which then combines with our current state to create a reaction. Here's a basic outline:

1. An external event occurs.

2. We notice it through our five senses.

3. The brain quickly deletes, distorts, or generalizes the information in order to process it without getting overwhelmed.

4. An internal representation is created.

5. Meaning is applied to that representation (image).

6. Our internal state at that moment (physiology plus previous representations) combines with the meaning we've applied to the event.

7. We react.

Step three, where the inner computation takes place, is central to the process. The world we see—deleted, distorted, and generalized—is not so-called reality, but our minds think it is, and that's really what matters. Our representation of the world determines what we see and therefore the options we have. Muggsy saw many options where most people would not see any, at least not any positive ones.

Muggsy's filter transformed adversity into a positive. "To the outside world, I'll focus on the good things," he says. "I have learned that there are always plenty of positive things if you pay attention to them. That's why, even with all the hardship, I can also honestly say that I had great times in the projects." What gets your attention gets you. Muggsy found gratitude in the ghetto.

Everyone has his or her own filter, and it is through this filter that we perceive the world. This filter—your map of the world—is based on the beliefs your mind has developed over the years from the meaning it assigned to each event in your life. It's completely biased. That's why two people can live through the same event and have totally different experiences. Because it's the only filter and process we've ever had, we don't even notice it. It's just life.

A person's perception of the world is only a map, not reality. It doesn't need to be reality and certainly would make things difficult if it were. Our visible spectrum is limited to seven colors—we cannot see what eagles or owls can, nor can we hear what a leopard or lop-eared rabbit hears. Radio waves and electricity are continuously acting without our detection. Whole portions of the world are deleted from our senses.

⬍ Adjusting Your Filter

The brain learns to recognize patterns and remember them, whether they are helpful or not. Assumptions are made in order for us to process information without spending hours in deliberation. If we see the leg of an elephant, the brain quickly assumes that the leg is connected to the body of an elephant and to three other legs, two big ears, and a long snout. If I wree ot sracblme teh wrods ni tihs stnecne, yuo wulod siltl udenrtsnad waht I wotre if the first and last letters of most of the words were in the correct order. For most of us, the brain quickly snaps to the closest appropriate word and unscrambles the letters (to read: "If I were to scramble the words in this sentence, you would still understand what I wrote.") That's how optical illusions work, because the brain jumps to conclusions. This brain activity is very helpful for processing information, but it gives us problems in focusing.

For example, when we attempt to narrow our focus, the brain keeps wanting to jump to the surrounding environment. An opera singer wants to sing beautifully, but her brain wants to judge her performance as she sings or gauge how the audience will react. A baseball player wants to keep a simple mind when he's at bat and focus on one quality swing, yet his brain keeps wanting to analyze surrounding information and see more.

Maybe you just want to concentrate on a task, and there's a swirl of activity buzzing around you. The swirl is a strong distraction. You have difficulty concentrating because your brain is used to jumping to the bigger picture, not limiting itself to the smallest part of the action.

Here's a test you can try: Choose a painting or photograph on the wall, and look at only the bottom right corner of the picture. Try not to allow your mind to jump to the entire picture. Don't let it think of what's attached to the small part that you're viewing. It's difficult. Your brain is equipped to see patterns to help you out, not knowing that in performance you want to focus on the smallest element of the task, having only a general awareness of the bigger picture.

In other words, focus is enhanced when you can break down a given task into its most basic element and then draw a bead on that alone. If you are a golfer, make one good swing; if you are a salesperson, make one good sales pitch.

It's difficult because our brains have adapted pattern-seeking scripts. Generalization is one of those scripts. Generalization is the process by which we "learn" from experiences and apply that learning to similar events in the future. It gives us a frame of reference. The problem is that it can go too far. We develop preconceived ideas—our own personal prejudices—that form beliefs about what should or will happen. For example, if you speak poorly and fumble for words at an important presentation, then you may generalize that you will always have problems getting your point across in that context. Generalization is helpful in that our brains try to learn from each situation, but the learning is skewed by our own bias. Generalizing is a useful process that allows us to use information from the past and project the future, but it can also be misleading. Just because you performed poorly at a certain venue does not mean you will perform poorly the next time you go there.

As opposed to generalization, deleting is a computation in which we pay attention to some aspects of experience and not to others. This process is a crucial element in performance, as multiple things are often going on at any one time, and so the performer must focus on the task at hand and not engage in anything else. We perform our best when we eliminate excessive thoughts and let our intuition take over during the moment of execution. The problem we run into with deletion is that we miss opportunities with the narrowed vision.

The third primary process in which we filter the data coming through our senses is distortion. In a negative frame of mind, for example, we notice any little negative and overemphasize the meaning. A small bump in the road becomes, "Today's just not my day," or "I can't catch a break." Perhaps at work your boss ignores you. You think, "My boss ignored me, therefore he's angry at me," but the reality is that he may have been preoccupied, depressed about a personal issue, or any number of possibilities. We perceive an event and attribute a cause or meaning when we don't actually know the real cause.

When you get frustrated, anxious, or depressed, often it's because in your model of the world you do not see suitable options. Self-actualizers respond creatively to stress because their model of the world has a wide range of options. When you make poor decisions or let your emotions get the best of you, you actually did the best you could with the options you had. The solution is to gather more resources. In other words, when you're angry, frustrated, or depressed, the best stance is to have multiple options that can turn around your negative state. The primary resource everyone has is the imagination.

As a kid, you learned to put imagination to use. Unfortunately, many people lose that ability as they "learn" about logic and reality. Knowledge, as Einstein said, is limited, but imagination encircles the world. Self-actualizers have learned how to put a positive spin on the events in their lives in order to create the emotions they want. For example, watching a fireworks display could really be watching a celebration of achieving your goals—in your imagination, the show was put on especially for you. Likewise, getting laid off means you'll get a better job. Whatever happens, neutral events and circumstances that you can't control are "what's supposed to happen" when you put a positive spin on things. There are often hidden positives in seemingly neutral or negative events, so consider what could be great even though you cannot see it. In the human imagination, the ordinary becomes extraordinary.

When you have a challenging long-term goal, you need to have constant reminders that focus your attention on the goal and the process of achieving it. Essentially there are two major concepts to be reminded of: your long-term dream (the feelings you want) and your long-term goal (the external outcome). Your long-term goal should remind you of your short-term goals (what you want to do today), and the same goes for your long-term dream. Long-term dreams, in one sense, are always the same for everyone, and that is to find resonance and Zoë. Likewise, your short-term goal, at its most basic form, is also always the same, and that is to be fully present.

Goals are unique because they're creations in your mind that you don't have yet. Thus your subconscious goes back and forth between what it "knows" about your past and your most dominant thoughts of today in order to create your belief about that goal. If your goal is a challenging one, the Trickster will continually remind you of past failures, so you need a plan to override that negativity. What helps are tools that can shift negative thoughts and images to positive, successful ones.

Here are a few ways to counteract negative thoughts:

1. Dismiss the thought immediately, knowing that a thought has power only by what you give it, and you give it power by letting it linger.

2. Replace the thought with the opposite thought or a similar affirmation. (For example, "I'm terrible at _____" becomes "I'm great at _____.")

3. Shout, "Stop!" in your head, and see an oversize red stop sign or see the giant letters S-T-O-P written across a blackboard.

4. Snap yourself back to the present. Wear a rubber band on your wrist, and snap it each time a negative thought enters your mind.

Negative thoughts are strongest when we fail, or when we feel that we did. In those moments of vulnerability, we must be prepared to handle the negative thoughts that will come and that could escalate into further mistakes or problems. Jim Fannin has what he calls the five-second rule: "You are only as good as the five seconds after every performance. Once the performance has been completed, the next five seconds will provide an opportunity to make a deposit or withdrawal from your bank account of optimism." He goes on, "The key to sustaining the zone state is to not go back into the past."

As an example, when baseball superstar Alex Rodriguez strikes out, he says, "I hit solid with an accelerated bat head" within five seconds of the strikeout. After every "failure," the mind wants to judge the performance as bad. The Trickster wants to say, "I told you so," and if we're not careful, those thoughts will have sufficient power (because we allow them to linger) to attract more negative thoughts, change our state, and internalize the failure (we feel like a failure).

What is really powerful is to learn how to change our state (as discussed in Chapter 5) so that we are not enslaved by our emotions. Then we can stay on the course toward our goals and dreams. We need to create a consciousness of those goals and dreams such that they are always near the front of our minds. Decathlete gold medalist Bruce Jenner, for example, installed a forty-two-inch hurdle in his living room that he cleared as many as twenty-five times a day.

Every time he did that, he put an image in his mind of hurdling and the success that would come.

As we learn to change our state to a consistently positive one, focused on our dreams and goals, we are better able to change how we see the world. Changing how we see the world is how we initiate a change in beliefs. A new belief is a re-association of how we see things.

Changing beliefs is largely a matter of continually changing your state to match that of the belief you want—until one day it clicks, and a complete re-association occurs. If you completely match the future state of what you desire, then desire turns into peace, confidence, and whatever feeling your desire gives you when you attain it. As you continue to do this it becomes a belief.

You Can Change Your Beliefs

University of Texas softball star Cat Osterman threw a nasty drop ball to Callista B. and struck her out for the ninth time in nine tries since the start of the season. The Women's College World Series (WCWS) was under way, and Osterman, one of the best pitchers to ever play the game, was once again throwing a no-hitter, with Callista another casualty. Texas was one of the favorites to win it all, relying on the dominant left arm of the team's masterful pitcher. In the sixth inning a runner walked and stole second base. Osterman walked the next batter to get to Callista, only to give up the game-winning hit as Callista's team went on to win the WCWS.

For Callista, as with Lewis Gordon Pugh, there seems to have been a dramatic shift in consciousness somewhere along the way.

Lewis had two major failures days before his world record, and Callista had nine failures in a row against the same pitcher. Then in the biggest at bat of her life, she got the game-winning hit off Osterman when no one else could hit her. What had shifted?

Their perceptions shifted. Their states changed. Beliefs can and do change all the time. Callista did it by creating a connection with what she wanted to achieve and continually shifting negative thoughts into positive, successful ones. She affirmed and visualized her goals daily. In the preseason she had begun visualizing the exact scenario that came up, and she did it just about every day for months. The scenario she visualized? With Cat Osterman pitching, the game-winning run on second base, and the World Series on the line, she gets the game-winning hit. Callista said that when they were walking the batter to get to her, she was filled with confidence. Then, when she was on first base, all she could think about was how she had visualized this for months and, sure enough, it all came true.

Affirmations

What Callista did was create a picture in her mind, one that seemed far-fetched at the time, and continually affirm that picture. Affirmations are statements about yourself regarding how you'd like to be in the future, as if it were true today. They should be stated in the positive ("I am," versus "I never" or "I don't") and fairly short. Here are some of her affirmations:

- I am the team MVP [most valuable player—she was!].
- I am a dominating, powerful hitter.

- ◆ I am smooth and flawless in the field.
- ◆ I love pressure—the more intense, the better I play.
- ◆ I am an incredible two-strike hitter.
- ◆ I control my destiny.

Of course, this was all in conjunction with her tremendous effort at practice and in the weight room, as well as learning to be present on and off the field. Callista's mind regularly took her to June, visualizing playing in front of the huge crowd, on national TV, with the pressure on, getting the game-winning hit. She had a script written out (before the season started) for her interview with the reporter after the game, asking her to talk about the big hit and how she was able to finally break through, along with her answers for each question. The script helped her visualize in detail the scene of her success. (We go over this in Chapter 8.) Callista continually visualized herself in the locker room after the World Series. When the actual event arrived, she had visualized it unfolding a certain way so many times, with the accompanying feelings, that she got those same feelings again during the game.

You don't have to believe your affirmation when you begin. In fact, it's most likely that you will not truly believe it; if you did, you would not need to affirm it—it would already be a part of your consciousness. The reason you are affirming it is to make it into a part of your consciousness, and this effort requires a planned attack, working on it daily, just as if you were training your body.

One of the most powerful techniques for changing your beliefs is to model someone who has the belief that you want to have. If you can see the world the way that person does, you can learn to believe in the same way that he or she believes. For any situation, you can ask yourself, "What does [the person who's best in the world at this] believe about himself regarding this sort of thing?" "What does she repeatedly say to herself?" Maybe your affirmation is, "I am an inspiring public speaker," but right now you are scared to death of public speaking. You may ask yourself how Winston Churchill felt when he gave a speech, or Barack Obama, or anyone else who appears to be an especially confident speaker. Then you can imagine that you feel what your role model would feel.

The ideal is to have three or so main affirmations posted where you will see them every day, and rotate them occasionally. The bathroom mirror (to be read while you brush your teeth) is a good place, as is anywhere that promises regular visibility.

Here are some powerful affirmations we all can use:

- **Something incredible is happening.** This statement directly counters the deceptions of the Trickster and the Critic. Sometimes amazing things are happening, in the best possible manner, but we just can't see them.
- **I live in a world of abundance.** This affirmation helps us to be grateful and attract positive energy.
- **Extraordinary opportunities pursue me daily.** There are endless opportunities that we can't see, and since we can't see them, it's easy to assume they're not there.
- **Every day, I'm getting better in every way.**
- **My body is a fit, powerful machine.** We're often too quick to say, "That's my bad leg," or "That's my weak side," and the subconscious just wants to make our beliefs real. When I tore my Achilles tendon a few years ago, I was really down and thinking negatively. One day I grabbed a magic marker and wrote on my cast: "My body is an incredibly powerful healing machine." My leg healed in record time.

- **I feel amazing.** Whenever you're not feeling positive or confident, act as if you are. Stand tall, stick out your chest, look up,
  and say this affirmation to yourself.

When you're standing in line or whenever you have spare time,
if your mind is clear and your heart is free, your thoughts will drift
toward an image of your goal, an affirmation, or some other positive
idea. You won't always be affirming your goal (though you will much
of the time); sometimes you'll just relax, but there's a big difference
between relaxation and boredom. Boredom makes you susceptible
to negativity, but there is little boredom when you have a big goal
and really want to live a passionate and challenging life.

As your consciousness gets more and more in tune with your
long-term goals and dreams, putting a positive spin on neutral
events will become natural. If you repeat your affirmation like a
mantra while you're standing in line or waiting in traffic, you'll find
that your energy will change.

 ## The Final Piece to Beliefs

One common hindrance to achieving your goals is a subconscious
belief that reaching a certain goal will affect you negatively in some
area of your life. For instance, say your goal is to be a famous athlete
or president of the company. How will achieving that goal change
your life? You'll likely have a lot of money, celebrity, and status. Does
that outcome conflict in any way with your values? If you happen to
feel that being financially wealthy is a bad thing, you may subconsciously sabotage your goal in order to preserve your values. An athlete may routinely get injured before big events if he or she harbors a

subconscious belief that winning those events is not congruent or is undeserved.

Take trying to quit smoking as an example. One reason many smokers struggle to quit is that there is a secondary gain they get from smoking. For many smokers, the habit is a social activity: they belong to a group with a common bond that perhaps they would lose if they were to quit. The nicotine, therefore, is only part of the equation.

In order to expand your beliefs, it's important to make sure the person you'll become and the life you'll live when your goal is achieved are congruent with your values. What your goal is doesn't matter as much as whether every part of you really wants it. What will achieving this goal give you? What will that give you?

As you learn to manipulate the images in your mind, you'll learn to change the world in which you live. You are in charge of the story line. How will it unfold? Is your world flat? In some way or another, everyone has limiting beliefs, but you can change yours if you want to.

 ## The Delancey Street Foundation

Alan Deutschman's book *Change or Die* relates the story of the Delancey Street Foundation, in San Francisco. Delancey Street is an organization that runs award-winning, multimillion-dollar businesses. The organization is extraordinary, and not just in relation to its success. All employees live together in a communal building. They also are all convicted criminals, and most are drug addicts. The average employee arrives illiterate and unskilled, never having held a job for more than six months. Every drug addict has to quit "cold turkey" upon entering Delancey, and the minimum stay is two years. No outsiders work for Delancey. Residents "police" themselves, and the organization accepts no money from the government. Mimi Silbert, CEO, is the only nonconvict. She also lives in the facility and draws no salary. How do they do it?

Silbert, who has Ph.D. degrees in psychology and criminology, is an expert at developing people. Chief among her abilities is getting people to feel what it's like to be successful. She asks these violent criminals, who arrive with severely limiting beliefs, to "act as if" they believe they could become caring, productive citizens. She teaches them how to respect and care for each other and, especially, to take responsibility for their actions.

Employees teach skills to each other, and—perhaps most of all—they gain a purpose beyond themselves. Each man and woman is taught that "though no one can undo the past, we can balance the scales by doing good deeds and earning back our own self-respect, decency, and a legitimate place in mainstream society." Even the bottom 5 percent of society, as Silbert lovingly refers to the residents she calls her family, can achieve extraordinary goals with hope and a dream. Slowly each day, as they gain more of the feel of what it would be like to reach their goals, they transform into the people they want to become.

The world *is* flat if you believe it is. It may as well be, because you'll never venture far enough to discover the truth until you change your belief. People all *knew* the world was flat in years past, until explorers challenged prevailing beliefs and found out otherwise. The reality you create in your mind is all that matters, in performance and in your daily life. As we continually learn to expand our beliefs, as Muggsy did, we must also learn to use our new abilities by being fully engaged in the present moment, where all extraordinary success happens.

Key Points from Chapter 6

- Beliefs are habits of behavior and expectation that are formed from how we interpret the events in our lives.
- Your beliefs come from your repeated feelings and experiences, and your beliefs attract more experiences to match those beliefs.
- We each have our own filter through which we view the world. We can control our experiences by adjusting this filter.
- You can change your beliefs by continually changing your state to match that of the belief you want. If you continually model how someone else thinks and feels, you can match the person's beliefs.
- Beliefs create a comfort level of what's possible and what's not. This process provides a range of performance and expectation for the subconscious to try to stay within.
- Learning to recognize negative thoughts and replace them with affirmations is a powerful way to help change your beliefs.

Follow-Up Questions and Activities

- Examine your beliefs about your goals. Pick a goal, and write down three beliefs you have about reaching it. Are those beliefs empowering? What do you have to change to achieve your goal?
- What do you need to do to get the feeling of success necessary to create a belief that your subconscious will relentlessly pursue?
- Practice observing your thoughts without judging them. What kind of patterns did you find?

- Wear an elastic band around your wrist, and snap it every time a negative thought lingers in your head. Then replace that negative thought with a positive thought.
- Write out, in full detail, a newspaper or Internet article about yourself as if your goal had come true.
- Post photographs and affirmations of your goals and dreams on your walls where you will see them every day.

A Clear and Present Beauty

*The Four Most Powerful
Ways to Be Fully Present*

*The true worth of a man is measured by the objects he
pursues.*

—**Marcus Aurelius**

Guglielmo Marconi connected a few
wires, around the start of the twen-
tieth century, and sent a message
across the Atlantic that changed history. He
enabled people to hear each other via radio
waves—but what did he really do? Marconi,
and Benjamin Franklin before him, only
tapped into what was already there. He did
not invent radio waves, just as Franklin did
not invent electricity. Radio waves and electrical currents were always there, always
available, just waiting for us to get in tune
with and connect with their energy. So it is
with beauty, focus, and presence—they are
always there, regardless of personal experience, patiently waiting for you.

Beauty is everywhere. Does the sun ever stop shining? Do the mountains ever cease reflecting glory? The abundance of beauty is never-ending, yet it's so easy to get caught up with the obstacles that overshadow all that's possible, that hide the amazing that awaits.

Our pursuit of achievement often leads to impatience. We want success and we want it now. We chase after goals, immersed in activity, looking for ways of doing things better, faster, and more easily. Then we hit roadblocks and get knocked down. We pick ourselves up, get rolling again, and get hit again. Sometimes the blocks are big and heavy and become brick walls. Most of us turn back dejected, but a few grab some rope and climb the wall. Those who persevere may have a limited line of sight, but their vision is still expansive, their eyes above the horizon as they climb. They are the ones who have learned to be fully present amid the adversity. In this chapter we will look at how to elevate our consciousness so we can transcend our circumstances and be fully present.

The ultimate aspiration, Zoë, is absolute fullness of life. Zoë has great experiences that take our breath away, moments when the mind and body are connected so perfectly that the task is effortless. These moments of freedom and creativity are enabled by our being fully present. To be fully present is to be fully engaged in the moment, fully experiencing it. The more present we become, the less we recoil from adversity, because we can see more opportunities and blessings in the struggle. Perhaps we'll see blessings *because* of the struggle. Being fully present paves the way for resonance, in which your mind and body are so organically connected and engaged that everything else falls away.

It's easy to lose touch with those feelings as we become numb in our busyness. Our single-minded pursuit of a better life has gripped us with the anxiety that comes from putting our trust in that which is unstable. The power of a single-minded pursuit must be directed toward something more stable and permanent. As we rid ourselves of what's not us, as Michelangelo did with David, we can shed the attachments and self-consciousness and get in tune with the beauty around us. That gives us the freedom to explore life's experiences with fresh eyes.

Here are four ways to be fully present:

- Have a simple mind.
- Tune in to beauty.
- Accept this moment.
- Be aware of your humanity.

Before expanding on these four concepts, let's get clear on what it is to be fully present.

 ## The Power of Full Engagement

When we're fully present, time often seems to slow down, movements become effortless, awareness is heightened, and we may even feel as if we're spectators watching everything unfold. Artists, musicians, and athletes have all described moments like that. Andy R., a national champion in golf and professional singer, described singing opera: "It's like playing golf. I want to be one with the moment and get beyond the actual task. In one particularly transcendent concert I was giving, I almost passed out. Not from fear or nervousness, but from being so removed from my body as to have temporarily forgotten I was even onstage." To be fully present is to reach a higher level of consciousness, a more powerful vibration of energy. Figure 7.1 shows

Figure 7.1 **The Expansive Power of Being Fully Present**

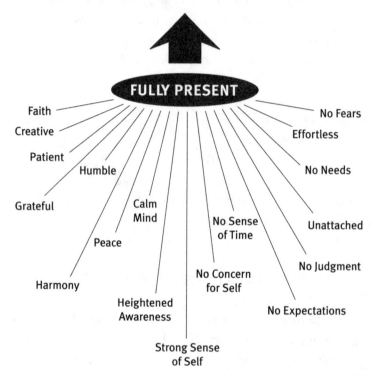

various elements of being fully present and the positive energy that results: swagger, focus, relaxation, enjoyment, and discipline.

In performance, desire is a powerful motivator. It pushes us to be disciplined and do the work that needs to be done in order to improve. Desire, however, can also prevent us from giving our best performances if it is not controlled. We really want to be successful, but for that to happen, we must be so focused in the moment of performance that desires fade away. Don't confuse desire with passion. Passion is found in the present, while desire looks to the future.

Desire is focused on something you don't have yet. It's a state of lack that has a different energy from the energy that comes with actually having what you want. Judgment often follows desire. Because you desire a certain outcome, you are constantly judging whether that outcome will materialize or not. When you're present, however, your goal is a successful outcome, but your focus is absolute in the moment. Thoughts have diminished to the point where desires have moved to the subconscious, with the outcome no longer a concern.

Imagine Tiger Woods lining up a ten-foot putt that would win a major tournament. In the moment of execution, he, as well as the rest of us, would perform best with a clear mind and an unburdened heart. The desire for the ball to go into the hole is not part of a clear mind—it's a thought wishing to control the future, which cannot be completely controlled. The time to look into the future is before the shot, visualizing the ball going into the hole. During performance, there are no thoughts about the outcome whatsoever when you're fully present. Legendary martial artist Bruce Lee put it this way: "The great mistake is to anticipate the outcome of the engagement; you ought not to be thinking of whether it ends in victory or in defeat."

Take the case of a salesman working on commission who needs to close a deal in order to pay the rent. He really wants the sale. Now he has a problem. His fervent desire to make the sale can significantly hurt his chances of actually doing so. His attachment to what he wants but can't control can easily make him needy. It's like asking someone on a date: if you really, really like that person, and he or she sees that, you may seem desperate. Whether you're selling yourself or selling vacuum cleaners, to be your best is to not be attached to whatever happens with your sales pitch.

Desires and expectations clutter the mind, and a cluttered mind always translates into doubt. Even a mind filled only with good thoughts can be detrimental. Clutter is the enemy of clarity. To reduce the clutter, it's helpful to simplify, to narrow down the essence of what you're doing. If you examine your best performances, you'll probably notice qualities such as confidence, relaxation, enjoyment, and discipline, all of which helped you pursue and attain some level of presence. If you had to narrow it all down to the most important factor in peak performance, you would find, I believe, that it is your ability to be fully present. More specifically, it would be your ability to feel how you want to feel in each moment of the performance. This is also the key in every area of your life.

> The ultimate goal of karate lies not in victory or defeat but in the perfection of the character of its participants.
>
> —Gichin Innakoshi, karate founder

Have a Simple Mind

To be fully present is to fully experience the moment. We cannot have the complete experience, however, if we set our minds on too many things. A mind can process only one thought at a time, and if there's a backlog, things get jammed up. Thoughts need to be filtered, desires need to be channeled (into being present), and the unconscious needs to have focused direction for optimum results. Philosopher Dietrich Bonhoeffer wisely wrote, "Your heart has room for only one all-embracing devotion."

Resonance is the powerful energy that emerges when your heart and mind connect, fully engaged in the moment. When you feel resonance, you're confident and centered, connected and congruent with your true self. It's a feeling of harmony and integrity, which sets the stage for not only extraordinary performances but also incredible experiences. To feel resonance is to experience the world "fully, vividly, selflessly, with full concentration and total absorption," as Abraham Maslow described the self-actualizers. Resonance is a powerful devotion.

One way to pursue resonance is to seek a simple mind. Stay focused solely on the moment or the task at hand, with positive, efficient thoughts. Narrow your task down to its smallest element. If you're washing dishes, wash one dish, and do it well; then do the next dish. If you're working out in the gym, do one repetition well (with your thoughts on the muscles you're working and proper form) and then the next. If you're writing, do as Hemingway said: write one true sentence. The focus is not on the past or future; the focus is on the most basic element of the current task. In sum, whatever you decide to do in the next moment is the most important thing in the world right then.

If you experience anxiety and frustration, or find yourself thinking about the past or future (unless you're visualizing, learning, or remembering something good), you've lost focus. Resonance comes from simplifying everything down to its smallest component and then controlling that component to the best of your ability. There are so many things out of your control that your mind is bound to wander off. When it does, you must gently but swiftly bring it back to the present.

Colorado Rockies performance coach Ronn Svetich remarks on what it means to have a simple mind while pitching. "I create a simple mind by being in control of what I can control, and what I can control is a simple mind," he says. "A simple mind is to get the sign [which pitch to throw] from the catcher, see the pitch in your mind, and then throw it. When you're starting to think about the umpire, the score, the base runners, the batter, your simple mind is lost." Those other factors are things to be aware of intuitively, not things to analyze between pitches. He tells his pitchers, "Your goal while pitching is to have a simple mind. Throw one quality pitch. When you come back to the dugout between innings, ask yourself, 'Did I keep a simple mind at least 80 percent of the time?' If you did, now ask yourself what you have to do to keep this simple mind. If you didn't, if some distraction took you out of the present moment, ask yourself what you have to do to get back your simple mind."

It doesn't matter if you write books, sell shoes, or strike out batters for a living: you perform your best when you're fully present. To be fully present and bring your best to each moment is to reduce conscious thinking and let your intuition take over. Your subconscious has access to far greater wisdom and mind-body connection than your conscious thinking. A great performer visualizes, affirms, and prepares for an event and then allows the subconscious to take over during the performance.

The path toward single-minded focus requires self-awareness in order for you to recognize the Monkey Mind's chatter. It's "normal" (and I use that word lightly here) to be focused on more than one thing, but remember that the mind can process only one thought at a time. Multitasking dilutes the focus as it skips around. It's typical to let the mind ramble and wander. We need to listen closely to our thoughts so that we can slow down the pace and even turn off all thoughts when need be. Because thoughts are so compelling, we need to be able to embed the best ones and disengage from the worst.

How can you detach from your thoughts? One way is to use some of the techniques from Chapter 6 to stop the negative thoughts. Getting centered, of course, is also a powerful way to let your thoughts go. You can also disassociate by becoming the observer: imagine being a neutral bystander, simply observing your thoughts and feelings without judgment. Say, for example, something has irritated you. Close your eyes and imagine yourself floating up above and noticing the source of your irritation and your reaction to it. You may also use the disassociation exercise from Chapter 5 and float high into the universe. Here are a few more ideas that may help you detach from anxious thoughts:

- Nothing is good or bad except thinking that makes it so (in regard to your circumstances).
- The actual source of your irritation is not the external event or person, but your reaction to it.
- Everything is here to teach you or help you; there is no randomness.

These three ideas (presuppositions) do not need to be 100 percent true to be of value. If you carry them with you as your beliefs, you'll be more present, you'll increase your awareness, and your learning will accelerate.

Another powerful presupposition is that you are forever attracting to yourself conditions and circumstances that best fit your predominant thought patterns. If you are continually annoyed, frustrated, and angry, those are all your choices, and those choices will attract more annoyance, frustration, and anger. As you learn to adjust your filter to perceive your circumstances more objectively and with more clarity, you'll create gaps in the flow of negative thoughts. In those gaps you can find peace. With peace you can simplify your mind and your focus. Thoughts are real forces, but they have no power except what you give them. You give them power when you let them linger, as if they're true.

Your mind wants to do one thing most of the time, and that is to bring the past with you. It's always running a monologue in your head that needs to be recognized and controlled. You are not your past. Nevertheless, it's difficult to not be dominated by it. Anybody who has failed a couple times in a row knows that. With each failure, the Trickster throws in its two cents of negativity, and slowly we begin to believe it more and more. Those repeated thoughts turn into beliefs if we're not careful.

With practice, the Monkey Mind can be transformed into a simple mind. Then you'll savor the solo moments, because now your imagination, clear and spacious, can produce great thoughts. Great performers have great imaginations. If your mind is clear, it's available to sense and connect with the good energy around you.

Perfect moments occur with little or no thinking. Thinking is the distraction, the slowing down of intuition, the secretarial guard that stops the poetic flow of mind-body connection. In our efforts to be fully present, we are impeded by the conscious mind. We need to know how to get past the conscious mind, the gatekeeper to the unconscious, so that we can connect with the beauty of and be totally immersed in great moments.

Tune In to Beauty

A simple mind is attracted to beauty—and beauty can override your current feelings. Maybe you can recall a time when you encountered unexpected beauty, perhaps a stunning sunset or an inspiring scene in a movie that took your breath away. However you were feeling in that moment changed in an instant as you connected with that powerful energy. You may think those moments are rare, but you can increase their frequency. Often you may get down because all you see is rain (especially growing up in Seattle as I did). The problem is not that the sun stops shining, but that you cannot see its shine. There is never a lack of beauty, only a lack of vision.

Beauty exists even amongst the deepest anguish. As concentration camp survivor Dr. Viktor Frankl puts it, to be worthy of our sufferings is beautiful. We cannot control everything that happens to us, but we can control how we respond to it and how we perceive the situation. We always have that choice.

When you choose to focus your attention on beauty, your vision expands. Beauty is intimately connected with positive energy and creativity. One trait that distinguishes top performers is their ability to recognize patterns and opportunities more quickly and more often than everyone else. A master chess player can look at a chessboard and instantly find openings and opportunities and see moves far in advance. A novice will look at the same board and see nothing special. So it is with beauty: with practice you'll be able to see the excellence, grace, and wisdom in moments as you never have before. When you're more present, you'll see more connections and patterns in your work and career, as well as more connections and patterns of beauty.

Beauty often comes in small things. Maybe it's an unexpected smile, a call from a friend, or the meaning you find in seemingly unrelated objects. A blade of grass becomes beautiful when you see the color it provides the earth, the food for animals, the hiding places for ladybugs, or the contentment of a dog rolling on its back in the yard. The more you look for beauty, the more you will find.

As you practice getting connected to beauty, you'll be more creative, and more ideas will come. The ugliness that always used to obstruct your view will be a little more translucent. Problem solving, a daily endeavor everyone faces, is markedly enhanced with creativity. Creativity comes from clarity and connection to beauty, just as connection to beauty increases clarity. They feed on each other. Acting coach Konstantin Stanislavsky wrote, "Try to discover beauty everywhere: in every posture, position, thought, and scene. This exercise is very important. A creative person must be able to see and extract beauty from things which a noncreative person overlooks entirely; and he must see beauty first, not deformity."

To tune in to beauty, first you must embrace the immediate environment and establish a connection. Everything that is around you is meant to be here. Learn to accept it the way it is so that you can find clarity and see the beauty. When you resist what is, your mind cannot be clear. Recognize that for every situation you encounter, you bring your own preconceived ideas on how it should be, and usually it's different from what you expect.

I sat down at the beach one day with an athlete prior to the 2008 Olympic Games in Beijing. It was an important time to foster confidence and visualize the upcoming performance. We found as secluded a spot as possible, but we were in a public park, and other people were wandering nearby. Initially, I resisted their presence, not wanting interference, but a well-trained monk could certainly be present amid much more chaos than this, I thought. After all, circumstances dictate our level of presence only in relation to our ability to be present. If we are well skilled in being present, the environment and situation have little importance. So, we mentally embraced those around us, honoring their presence. The potential detractors blended into the trees and the breeze off the ocean, assimilating into our experience, which was powerful. Tuning in to beauty accesses the peace within us, which attracts positive energy in chaotic circumstances.

When you arrive at your workplace tomorrow, you'll doubtless be subjected to things that have annoyed you in the past. Perhaps it's the hum of the air conditioner, a noisy coworker, or a line at the copy machine. There are endless possible annoyances, and you have good reasons to be annoyed. Good reasons notwithstanding, if you embrace everything in your environment as if it were there to help you in some way—even if only to increase your patience—then your eyes will open to the positives that might have been hidden before. You'll also free up your mind for creativity. The problem is not the annoying event or person, it's your limited perspective.

Accept This Moment

Deepak Chopra once said, "There is a hidden meaning behind all events, and this hidden meaning is serving your own evolution." Chopra's words are powerful, not because they are always true, and they may not be 100 percent of the time, but because that belief helps you learn from adversity and see possibilities. It takes your focus to another level. To be fully present requires embracing everything that's in your life right now and not resisting your circumstances. This precept does not mean that everything is good (some things are inherently evil), nor that you should quit discerning between right and wrong. It simply means that you should accept that which you cannot change; don't resist it. Embrace your life as it is right now.

What you don't have in this moment, you don't need. The idea is this: *Embrace everything that's happening to you, every person in your life, and every situation that you encounter—as if you chose it.*

> All of our invented fears involve either the past or the future; only love is in the present. Now is the only real moment we have, and love is the only real emotion because it's the only one that occurs in the present moment. Fear is always based on something that happened in the past and causes us to be afraid of something we think may happen in the future. To live in the present, then, is to live in love, not fear.
>
> —**Elizabeth Kubler-Ross**, *Life Lessons*

You may ask, "What if my circumstances are undesirable?" or "How will I get anywhere if I accept where I am right now?" It is a given that you will encounter circumstances you do not desire. Maybe you should ask, "How can I create better circumstances?" and "How can I reach my goals most efficiently considering where I am right now?"

It should go without saying that if a situation is undesirable, you will change it if you can. The problem lies in resisting what you cannot change. In such cases, inner peace, creativity, and happiness are diminished. When you are able to accept what you cannot change, your mind is free to seek creative ideas on how to improve the situation.

Resisting what's currently in your life is partly saying that you're not responsible for it. Not taking responsibility allows you to be a victim, which brings a lot of negativity. In contrast, if you believe that every circumstance and every situation is here to teach or help you, and that you attracted it, you can move into a state of peace and learning instead of constantly reacting to perceived threats. Then you can truly grow and improve. In your life story of how things should be, you may overlook the truth through your self-conscious glasses and be unable to appreciate the possibility that everything is unfolding exactly as it should. You can get caught up in the tangible world of circumstances and setbacks and easily dismiss the unseen world that controls the tangible world, the one always available in presence, focus, and beauty.

Judgment is the first form of resistance. When you label a situation in your life as bad, you automatically resist it. That's a mistake. Resistance creates counterresistance. The martial art of aikido, for example, blends your energy with the attacker's force, taking them where they want to go, instead of resisting. The most important aspect in your life, as well as in your performance, is not what happens to you; it is how you perceive and react to what happens to you. Chi Chi Rodriguez, one of golf's legendary performers, knew this when he said, "I never prayed to make a putt. I always prayed that I would react well if I missed."

Perhaps we should *pray not for our circumstances to change, but for the strength and courage to perceive our circumstances differently.*

Take a typical golfer: His tee shot flies far to the right, almost out of bounds. He instantly reacts negatively. How come? Because the ball didn't go where he wanted it to go. What if, however, the golfer were to free himself of the desire for the ball to go where he wants it to go? Then wherever it lands, the golfer can just walk over and play the next shot, instead of getting frustrated or anxious.

You may ask, "If something is really bad, should we not react appropriately to that bad event?" The operative question is actually, how do you know if it's inherently bad or good? Hitting the ball into the water, into the sand, or out of bounds is not morally good or bad. It's "bad" because something happened that you didn't want. Then again, is what you want always what's best for you? You can probably think of situations in your life in which you're glad you didn't get what you wanted, because something better happened that you didn't foresee.

Maybe hitting your ball into the sand trap is the best thing for you now, on the first day of the tournament, because you need to get used to the sand so that on the last day you can hit the winning shot from there. There could be lots of reasons why hitting the ball into the sand with this shot is the best outcome for you. You already know that adversity creates opportunity. You may recover with an incredible follow-up shot that generates enough confidence to last you throughout the tournament, leading your opponents to think, "Wow, there's no stopping her today."

We are constantly deceived by the particular story we create around a given situation. We judge each moment, label it good or bad, and then react emotionally to it. Our lives become one reaction after the other, and we never get closer to our goals. The truth is that if we live as if each circumstance in our lives is our teacher, we will see more beauty and find more greatness.

If we learn to pay attention, instead of constantly judging and resisting, we will see other options. We'll be able to connect seemingly unrelated thoughts so that they can serve us. In our attachment to comfort, happiness, and other desires, we are hard-pressed to accept two principal conditions that help us grow: discomfort and adversity. As we improve our ability to accept what is, we are improving our resistance to the Critic, which wants to judge everything. Judgment comes from attachment, and attachment leads to resistance. Acceptance comes from ridding ourselves of attachments.

The main attachment we humans have is to our self-centered lives. It's really an attachment to the symbols of our lives, to what we have, what we've done, and how we compare with others. If we can drop those attachments, we can live vividly and experience fully. This approach to life allows us to seek out our true selves and find real meaning.

Be Aware of Your Humanity

Driving along the Southern California coastline one summer evening, I pulled over to look at the ocean. The moon and stars lit up the rugged coast. I got out of the car and immediately was overwhelmed by the power of the ocean, which was roaring like a thousand lions along an endless veldt. I felt so minor, so inconsequential in the big picture. I was reminded of my humanity.

Often in our drive to achieve, we have a certain feeling of entitlement, thinking we deserve this and that, which leads to frustration, as expectations frequently do. Entitlement is a derivative of pride, the limiting kind, the one whose vocabulary has three words: look at me. People often confuse pride and confidence, because on the outside they look very similar. They are fundamentally different, however, in that pride is dependent on what we think others think about us, whereas confidence reflects how we feel within ourselves. The desire for pats on the back and superiority over others is pride that limits us, since it's out of our control and dependent on others, which increases self-consciousness.

Pride and entitlement combine with arrogance to provide the lifeline for the ego. When we are not aware of our natural self-centered tendencies, our vision, understanding, and self-awareness are critically restricted. Learning and growth, crucial in the pursuit of Zoë, get constrained by the ego.

We are all tested by the praise we receive. Compliments can be dangerous. If we accept them with grace and humility, they can encourage and inspire. A smile and a thank-you are all that is needed, and they are needed. One cannot maintain the swagger required for extraordinary performance without accepting, rather than deflecting, sincere, warranted compliments. The danger resides in the ego's self-consciousness.

Consider the *Sports Illustrated* cover "jinx." *Sports Illustrated*, one of the top U.S. sports magazines, puts photographs of the latest sports icon on its cover. This act alone frequently has an amazing impact on the athletes who are featured. Their performance often tends to hit a downward spiral. What happens, I believe, is that the athletes start to think excessively about their performance and how good they are. The minute they do that, they become self-conscious. And we know where self-consciousness leads. Extraordinary performance is the result of extraordinarily hard work, of integrating mind and body, learning to feel and not think, and developing the self-awareness needed to be present. Praise and media coverage always test our ability to stay in the moment.

Rick Pitino, head basketball coach at the University of Louisville, is the only men's coach in NCAA history to lead three different schools (Providence, Kentucky, and Louisville) to the Final Four. After thoroughly beating Arizona in the regional semifinal of the 2009 NCAA tournament, he said, "I think a lack of humility is the greatest killer of potential, so we are not going to fall in love with ourselves just because we had a good game tonight. We understand what we're up against."

Humility starts with gratitude. Gratitude reveals the beauty around you and brings positive energy. A sense of gratitude reminds you that there's a bigger story than you that's unfolding; you're here today, gone tomorrow. As you read this, mountains are forming, birds are migrating, penguins are marching, and polar ice caps are melting. When you're grateful, you create a sense of humility, and this empowers you. Humility should never be confused with a compromise of confidence. Humility connects you with others and taps into their good energy. It also opens you to learning and keeps you focused.

Ohio State football coach Jim Tressel (five-time Big Ten Conference champion, and counting) has his football players spend time in solitude every day. During that quiet time, each player must think of at least one thing for which he's grateful.

> Every man is my superior in some way, in that I learn from him.
>
> —Ralph Waldo Emerson

Gratitude and humility are important to an Ohio State football player. Tressel says, "If your most talented players are also your hardest workers, you've got a chance for real success, because everyone looks up to those guys who produce. And if those top players also have genuine humility, you really have a chance for something special."

Humility helps you see what's possible with others and expands your sense of self. Whereas pride blocks the ability to see the truth, humility recognizes your own ignorance. It sees the blinders of self-centeredness, and that alone broadens perspective. Your sense of self grows with more humility, as does your freedom, because there are no threats to defend. Learning is highest.

I flew to Coronado, California, the headquarters for the U.S. Navy Seals, the elite Special Forces unit, to interview some members as part of my research of top performers. I was spending the day with one instructor, Joe D., and I asked him if humility plays a role in being a Seal. His immediate answer caught me off guard: "Definitely. Humility can defeat any opponent. We may have to enter a building to kill a bad guy, and pride and false bravado will provoke busting down the front door, but that may get you killed. With humility you'll step back and see the situation clearly, and maybe you'll realize you need to slip in quietly through the back door."

Humility sees more of the big picture, whereas pride can make you careless. It can also get you killed. The samurai warriors cited in Chapter 4 could easily have allowed their egos to take over. Holding honor as a higher value than even their own lives, however, they couldn't risk the carelessness that giving in to ego would engender. Pride chips away at your true self as you let your ego build arrogance, leaving you constantly defending threats to your identity. Humility, however, creates room for learning and lays the groundwork for real confidence and inner peace.

Mimi Silbert, CEO of the Delancey Street Foundation, turns ex-cons into star businesspeople by teaching them to love and care for each other. Their "each one teach one" program helps each employee develop a sense of self and brings dignity and self-respect to their lives. The philosophy at Delancey is based on whole-life learning, teaching each employee various vocations as well as the basic skills of honesty, integrity, and service to others. Egos stay in check because even the CEO doesn't draw a salary. Silbert's outstanding team at Delancey has shown the world what's possible when you have a purpose beyond yourself and the courage to stay present when everything within you and society around you try to keep you in the past.

One of the most formidable enemies of presence is busyness. The articulate Trappist monk Thomas Merton said, "Busyness is the most pervasive violence . . . it kills the inner root wisdom that leads to a fruitful life." In our busyness we lose our true selves with our inability to be present; we eventually become numb to all around us, beauty and everything else. To be fully present takes time—there is no other way.

Just as time-outs are called in sports, you need to take time-outs in your life in order to be present. When you're at work, trying to multitask, consumed by deadlines, and on the verge of being overwhelmed, there is always clarity that awaits. If you don't take time to sharpen the saw, as author Stephen Covey suggests, your productivity decreases. There must be gaps in the busyness, ideally every ninety minutes. Just listen. Look and really see. Feel. Find solitude. When you make it a point to take scheduled sections of time each day to listen, look, and feel, you will develop a sense of curiosity and wonder. In doing so, you will also find more gratitude, humility, and reverence. This experience alone is empowering.

When you have reverence, you're more intentional with your actions and attentive with your eyes. You'll see more. Maybe you'll keep track of your thoughts and feelings in a journal. If you want to develop self-awareness, a journal is a useful tool. It shows you who you are and helps you see the rich experiences of life, especially the low points that teach us so much. True gratitude and humility are present only when you stop and really see, feel, and recognize all that you have been given to arrive here, as well as all that awaits you tomorrow—even if tomorrow never comes. Self-consciousness and attachments are nonfactors when you're fully present.

In your quest for extraordinary performance, make sure your desires are taking you where you want to go. If you aspire to absolute fullness of life, then focus your desires on love, wisdom, and courage. You'll develop a presence that will help you perform under pressure—as you'll see in the next chapter—and teach you how to live.

Key Points from Chapter 7

- ◆ To be fully present is to be completely engaged in the moment, fully experiencing it, with no needs, no desires, and no thoughts of the outcome.
- ◆ Four guidelines help us to stay present: have a simple mind, tune in to beauty, accept this moment, and be aware of your humanity.
- ◆ In our busyness, we become numb to our senses and lose out on the creativity, insight, and dreams that come with being present.
- ◆ When you embrace what you cannot change, you free yourself to find opportunities.
- ◆ Resonance occurs when you're fully present, using your gifts, and challenged in something you love.

Follow-Up Questions and Activities

- ◆ Observe your level of presence throughout the day. Notice times when you're frustrated, angry, depressed, or daydreaming. Keep an index card in your pocket, and check off the number of times during the day when you're not present.
- ◆ Practice detaching from your thoughts. Imagine you are a neutral bystander, or perhaps a researcher or journalist, observing your thoughts. How does the act of observing your thoughts affect those thoughts?
- ◆ Get in the habit of keeping a journal to collect data on your thoughts and feelings each day. How did those thoughts and feelings affect your ability to be present? You may start by listing a few things for which you're grateful. You may also simply

write phrases or just words—whatever comes to mind in your stream of consciousness.

- Pick one of the four ways that help us to be present, and focus on that guideline for one full day. Do the same for each of the other three. On the fifth day practice getting centered and present with any of the four ways whenever you notice you're not present.
- Practice taking time-outs, from as little as one minute to a full day, during which you work on being present and seeing more beauty.

Poise Under Pressure

Four Keys to Extraordinary Performance

The mind should be neither solemn nor agitated, neither pensive nor fearful . . . the will should not be heavy, but the depth of one's awareness should be.

—Miyamoto Musashi, samurai

Chesley Sullenberger made an announcement to the passengers and crew, ninety seconds before hitting the water: "Brace for impact." When U.S. Airways flight 1549 lost all power, the former fighter pilot said he experienced "the worst sickening, pit-of-your-stomach, falling-through-the-floor feeling" he had ever had.

Captain Sullenberger ("Sully") had three and a half minutes to accomplish what few commercial airline pilots had ever pulled off. He was trying to avoid the fate of an Ethiopian airliner that landed in the Indian Ocean in 1996 but broke into pieces and killed the majority on board. As Sully recounted all that needed to be done in order to survive—touch down at a descent rate just over minimum flying speed but not below it, keeping the wings exactly level and the nose slightly up, all simultaneously—he noted that his focus was absolute. "I thought of nothing else," Sully said after having landed safely in the Hudson River the morning of January 15, 2009. Despite the pressure of 155 lives in his hands in a situation that held a high probability of death, he said, "I was sure I could do it. The physiological reaction I had to this was strong, and I had to force myself to use my training and force calm on the situation." It wasn't a hard thing to do, he says. "It just took some concentration."

Sullenberger acted fearlessly in a moment of crisis. What about the rest of us? Is this something that can be taught? Definitely. Poise under pressure can be learned, as Sully himself did. Pressure comes from what we think about the situation, not from the situation itself. Tension and anxiety are the result of concern about a situation in which the outcome is not in our full control. It's very similar to the scenario that elite athletes seek: challenging situations in something at which they are talented and in which there is a good chance of failure. It's the essence of competition.

In this chapter we will discuss pressure and poise and where the two intersect. Shooting baskets in your backyard is one thing, but performing the same task in front of millions for a national championship is another. Discussing an exciting idea at work takes on new meaning when you go from presenting in front of your department to addressing a company-wide audience. We will look at not only the best way to think about pressure situations but also how to get yourself to be fully engaged in those situations (so you "think of nothing else") and how to feel the way you want to feel (and be "sure you can do it") when it matters most. Whether you're negotiating a deal with your career riding on it, about to perform your first brain surgery, or playing a game of chess, it's all the same: there's a task, there's what you think about the task, there's how you want to feel when you perform the task, there's your performance, and there's the outcome. Poise under pressure comes down to feeling how you want to feel during the performance. It's the feeling of resonance.

Resonance, the freedom and passion that come when we're fully present and congruent, feeds off the energy that pressure brings. Resonance and extraordinary experience are intricately linked, just as are poise under pressure and extraordinary performance. We all want to be confident and relaxed, focused and disciplined, and to have fun when we do what we do. (Recall the five characteristics that emerge from being fully present—see Figure 7.1 on page 138.) This chapter explains how to apply what we've learned so far to the pressure moments, when we want to bring our best.

The Essence of Poise

The dictionary calls *poise* a state of balance or equilibrium. Equilibrium occurs when we're fully present. In the routine moments of our lives, our minds are pulled in many directions. Endless bouncing between the past and future as well as incessant negative thoughts constantly threaten to drag us down. They create an underlying anxiousness that seems to accompany us in our lives. Occasionally that anxiety gets removed, for various reasons, such as spending time with good friends, getting caught up in a favorite hobby or book or movie, or perhaps finding that special state that comes when challenge meets talent and passion.

World-class performers and athletes describe the feelings of their best moments with words such as *effortless, relaxed, focused, heightened awareness, harmony*, etc. Each of these words illustrates the feeling of being fully present. Poise is the result of being able to direct your energy toward being fully present when you need it the most.

In equilibrium, there is a steady state of balance, and with poise, there is also peace. Equilibrium is the result of a clear mind and an unburdened heart, where there are no needs, expectations, desires, judgments, or concerns for self. Balance is off when you have needs, because "need" by definition is a state of lack. When your mind goes into the past or future, unless for a positive reason, equilibrium is off.

We live our daily lives under constant threat of disequilibrium. Things happen. Parking tickets. Missed appointments. Budget cuts. Unmet expectations. By themselves, those events do not affect our equilibrium. It's our reactions to the events that cause tension and anxiety. Often what hurts us the most is the fear of failing, which is neither present nor balanced. Perhaps the root cause is the desire to look impressive, or not to look foolish, both of which can become attachments that enslave us. Performance carries constant threats to equilibrium. In fact, it's the purpose of competition to create those threats that take us out of our comfort zones. Competition, whether in business or athletics, is built-in adversity to increase challenge and enjoyment. It ceases to be enjoyable, however, when we take our focus off the task and put it on the end result, where uncertainty resides (this we save for visualization).

If we can find a way to remove our attachments, we can shift away from tension and toward freedom and equilibrium. In my practice working with world-class athletes, teams, and businesses,

I've identified four keys to the poise that is necessary for extraordinary performance:

- Clear perspective
- Mastery orientation
- Positive rivalry
- Connection with the performance

Poise Key Number One: Clear Perspective

In the pursuit of the extraordinary, it's easy to get caught up in the outcome and lose sight of the process and the reason why you do what you do. Whether you're an accountant, an athlete, or an office manager, what is your ultimate purpose? What is the legacy you want to leave? If your identity is riding on the outcome, and you can't fully control that outcome, then anxiety and tension displace balance and equilibrium. For you to maintain a balanced state, failure must not define you. When you have a strong sense of self, failure doesn't define you because who you are is much more than any setback.

Sport psychologist Matt Brown explains:

> If you're a hockey player, but instead of defining yourself as a hockey player you recognize that you possess a set of qualities that cannot be taken away, then your "identity" cannot be taken away. "Who you are" takes on an enduring quality. "I'm athletic, physical, competitive, social, creative, aggressive, and intuitive, so hockey happened to be *a great fit for who I am*." An injury, getting cut from a team, retirement,

or a major performance setback—none of these things takes away the essence of who you are *unless* you've defined yourself by the activity and its outcomes. When you go to perform, if you're not fighting to protect an identity, then you can use *hockey* to connect to it. It's a medium to experience yourself, and the best way to do that is to surrender to the moment because the act of playing *is* the connection, not the outcome itself.

A clear perspective provides the stability needed to maintain equilibrium. When we lose confidence and get immobilized in fear, generally it's a loss of perspective. We have pushed passion and feeling aside to focus on an uncertain outcome. Confidence is a combination of trust and faith, where trust is confidence in the present and faith is confidence in the future.

Perhaps the most powerful pursuit, one that promotes trust and faith, is to learn, grow, and help others. A powerful perspective is humble and grateful, because it sees the big picture and what is truly meaningful. It knows the value of failure and suffering, rejecting neither, embracing both. Learning is the focus; winning is the byproduct. When you focus on learning and growth, you can better manage the discomfort and stress of pressure situations.

Dawn Staley, the Olympic gold medalist basketball player profiled in Chapter 3, played to win, but it's not *why* she played. She played for the incredible experiences she had on the court. Her dreams were in the playing, performing with passion and joy— whether she won was secondary. It's like Clara Hughes sending her Olympic medals to her mom (Chapter 1). Her medals are "not what provide the deep sense of accomplishment, which," she says, "fills my sense of self, in turn teaching me how to live." They both play to win but recognize that winning is not the reason they play, and this quality helps them perform with poise under pressure, which then puts them in a position to win. Winning was their goal, not their dream.

Dreams are feelings you can control; goals are outcomes you cannot (not completely). Living your dreams means experiencing the amazing feelings you get while you pursue your goals, such as passion and love and being caught up in the moment. It's not based on the outcome of your goal. Living your dreams means pursuing your biggest goals, setting smaller goals, and dancing along the way. It's loving what you're doing more than the outcome of what you're trying to do.

Bonnie Blair, the most decorated speed skater in U.S. history, had a perspective on her sport that allowed her to compete with passion and focus, unafraid of failure. At one Olympics she finished fourth in a race, but that result was more important to her than one of her gold medals, because it was her personal best in that event. Dr. Jim Bauman, U.S. Olympic team sport psychologist, talks about Bonnie Blair and other world-class athletes: "Their perspective about what they're doing and why they do it is just different. We just finished the Winter Games over in Torino [Italy]. We had people over there that really didn't necessarily compete for the gold medal and all the fame and fortune and da, da, da, da, da. They're really in it to see what they can get out of their own system."

A powerful perspective focuses on the experience more so than the goal. The goal may be to win a gold medal or reach a certain sales number, but the focus is on the moment-to-moment experience. Top performers who perform exceptionally and live balanced, fulfilling lives want challenges, and they want them to be meaningful. The rest is simply feedback.

Poise Key Number Two: Mastery Orientation

When your life has a clear purpose, your perspective switches from short-term gains, which seesaw up and down, to fulfilling that purpose. As a result, everything changes. No longer do you "have to" win this event, impress your boss, or make your quota.

Mastery is the endless pursuit of self-awareness and personal growth, where winning and achieving are the by-products. Each day has the same importance as the day before, with the same questions being asked of you: Can you be present and positive today in each moment, and see what that moment has to teach you? Can you be true to yourself when the world around you is trying to pull you every which way? Can you drop your attachments and listen and learn? If you want to achieve extraordinarily, remember this: all great work is first done within you.

Because mastery is focused on growth rather than outcome, it helps you to stay fixed on the process rather than jump to the end result. Mastery embraces suffering and failure, because mastery is the pursuit of self-discipline, self-awareness, and personal growth. Mastery does not obsess about results but rather focuses on the specific details of the process that move experience (and performance) from ordinary to extraordinary. Mastery transcends circumstances because it is not attached to the outcome.

The most impervious obstacle to seeking mastery is the ego. The ego is attached to the four tenets of the affluenza virus: money, possessions, achievements, and status. Mastery is the feeling of control, whereas the ego is controlled by results; mastery is freedom, and ego is tension and anxiety; mastery has few needs, while the ego is very needy.

Basketball coach Phil Jackson played in the NBA, where, he said, emotions and ego ruled his life. He was attached to winning and fearful of losing. Once he got into coaching, though, he saw the process differently. Jackson describes the fleeting nature of success: "Even as we're being handed the trophy to the NBA championship, we are no longer a success. The moment has passed." Mastery understands the human element of life, by which we can do everything right and still "fail," whereas the ego has no grasp of learning and growth.

Poise Key Number Three: Positive Rivalry

In 2005 Bode Miller became the first American in twenty-two years to win the overall World Cup in Alpine ski racing, following that up with another World Cup title in 2008. Bode loves to ski, and the greater the challenge, the greater the opportunity he has to push himself to the point where every part of his mind and body are intensely focused, deeply feeling the sport he loves. His definition of success seems to be based more on great experiences than on the outcome of the race. In one notable moment of Miller's career, he revealed a technical advantage to some international opponents (to the dismay of his U.S. ski team members) because he didn't want an unfair edge. It's like the guy who fights you tooth and nail in a race to the bottom of the mountain for a case of beer and then, after beating you, says he doesn't drink. He races to win, but more than that, he loves the race.

When Tiger Woods speaks of his opponents, he seems to enjoy when they do well. Hoping that your opponents will not have their "A" game not only generates negative energy but also is not sound strategy. For you to improve and play at your highest level, having a talented opponent who is playing in top form often gives you the maximum opportunity to do it.

Embracing your opposition as an essential component of your growth is a key part of, as Dr. Cal Botterill says, "keeping the *want to* greater than the *got to*." *Want to* allows you to perform with passion and freedom. *Got to* is restricting, because if you've got to win or get this sale but you cannot fully control it, there's no freedom.

> The opponent is not the enemy—they're our partner in the dance.
>
> —Phil Jackson

The word *compete* comes from the Latin *competere*, which means "to seek together; strive in common; coincide." True competition means two (or more) rivals are playing the game they love together. Great performers love competition in and of itself—it's an opportunity to feel alive.

If it's true that extraordinary performance is a subset of extraordinary experience, and I believe it is, then positive energy is important. If, in your quest to reach your goal, you focus on extraordinary experience—performing with passion and vividly experiencing the moment—you're giving yourself the best shot at extraordinary performance. When you see your rival as a component of your success rather than an impediment to it, you can maintain positive energy.

 ## Poise Key Number Four: Connection with the Performance

If there is one attribute that best reflects poise, it's the ability to be fully engaged in the performance and vividly experience it. It's that feeling of resonance that occurs when you're fully present (often in the midst of something you love) and intuition takes over. Poise comes from connecting with the performance in such a way that you become one with the action. The artist becomes the art. Movements are effortless, thoughts are minimal, and feel is maximized.

Resonance is the framework for poise and extraordinary experiences. When you have resonance in a pressure situation, that resonance is reflected as poise, which leads to extraordinary performances. Three conditions lead the way in connecting with your performance: physiology, emotional preparation, and visualization.

Physiology: Getting the Feel

You may recall that your energy, or state, is largely affected by your physiology, by the image in your mind, and by your desires. When you focus those three areas in a synergistic fashion, you can direct your energy toward your ideal performance state. Resonance is that state, and poise is the result of reaching it. We talked about how to control your physiology in Chapter 5. Now we'll turn to how physiology affects poise and resonance.

When you're doing something you love, you love it because you truly feel it. You can unite with this energy by learning to fully experience the feel of your body in the midst of competition or performance. Resonance is full of feeling, but not necessarily emotion. Although resonance can be strongly associated with happiness, it's more often associated with the feelings of clarity, challenge, and being fully present.

Often athletes, musicians, and even dancers notice that in moments of pressure, they have less physical sensitivity, perhaps diminished feeling in their hands or fingers, and are so nervous that they can't get a feel for the ball, the instrument, or the moves they need to perform. Fully experiencing your performance, in contrast, means performing with a heightened awareness—or, you could say, a heightened feel.

Developing awareness of the feel of your body in pressure situations is important for peak performance. Our North American way of life has desensitized us. Clutter has taken the place of clarity. We've lost the need for our senses in everyday life, and they've atrophied. Your ability to see, smell, feel, and hear needs to be rejuvenated, enough so that when you visualize, you can taste victory. We want to experience our senses so vividly that the imagination needs little effort to get back to that feeling when we re-create it in our minds.

It's an interesting paradox: on the one hand, extraordinary performances come with incredible feelings, but on the other hand, developing those moments requires discipline and control of your feelings and emotions. There is no poise without first clarity. Sorting through this interplay of emotion and feeling—the heightened awareness, confidence, relaxed intensity, performing to succeed but not fixated on success—takes a lot of work. It takes a commitment to learn about yourself. It's not easy, but it's well worth it. Doug Newburg, Ph.D., is a former University of Virginia basketball player who has conducted in-depth interviews with hundreds of elite performers, from professional and Olympic athletes to rock stars and surgeons. He studied what they had in common when they performed their best and how they developed their confidence and focus. His research resulted in five pertinent questions:

- ◆ How do I want to feel?
- ◆ What does it take to get that feeling?
- ◆ What keeps me from that feeling?

- ◆ How can I get it back?
- ◆ What am I willing to work for?

As you hone your ability to feel, you'll be able to create routines and a lifestyle that will put you in situations in which you have that feeling. All outstanding performers have routines that prepare them for game day. Tom Trebelhorn, Major League Baseball manager and coach, said he never managed a Hall of Fame athlete who wasn't meticulous and compulsive about his routines. They get to the park at a certain time, take a certain number of ground balls, listen to certain music—sometimes down to the minute. The trick with routines is to use them to help get the feeling of resonance, but whenever you are interrupted or cannot stick to your routine, tell yourself, "This is how it's supposed to be today." Accept this interruption as if you chose it.

To truly connect with the performance, we must learn to connect with confidence during the most pressure-filled situation. The best among us walk with a certain swagger. You can see it in the eyes, the posture, the confidence. Kevin Towers, general manager of the San Diego Padres, noted, "If I was scouting a prospect and did not know what he looked like, I could spot him walking off the bus just by how he carried himself." Those who are talented, and who know it, exude a certain energy common to all great performers.

Your swagger is the way you carry yourself when you feel so connected with your true self that no failure will lessen your confidence in who you are. A swagger is not arrogance, that false bravado inflicted with affluenza. It's walking tall because you know who you are, you love what you're doing, and you know how to connect with your performance. Here are a few habits that can help you to connect with your performance:

- Get centered and reboot when frustrated or not present.
- Walk with a swagger.
- Recite affirmations.
- Practice putting positive spins on your circumstances.
- Visualize your goals and dreams.
- Use a journal to review your thoughts, feelings, and performances.

Emotional Preparation: Ready for Anything

When Sullenberger's plane hit the birds that destroyed the airliner's engines, immediately he knew it was very bad: "My initial reaction was one of disbelief." The jumbo jet had lost all power over one of the most densely populated areas of the planet. Obviously Sully was surprised at the sudden life-threatening situation he was facing, yet instincts took over and he grew calm, focused, and confident. Sully had a consciousness of poise under pressure, which helped him prepare himself to handle anything.

The feelings you experience under pressure present extreme challenges in performance. Feelings are magnified in pressure situations, and unexpected events can throw you off balance quickly. Consider a situation in which you have a make-or-break presentation to give, and when you arrive at the site, there's no projector for your PowerPoint. All your notes are on the software. Immediately the Critic reacts with a negative response. It can instantly throw you off. In fact, endless possible glitches can disrupt your focus, but if you're emotionally prepared, you can adjust to anything.

Emotional preparation is the readiness to handle the doubts, anxiety, and fear that may come before a high-profile performance or when unexpected events or other adversity confront us. Nerves are energy we can use. They become a problem, however, when we react to our nervousness or fear with resistance. Much of the trouble with anxiety and fear is our resistance to it, which actually creates the problem, whereas accepting unwanted feelings allows them to fade. When we can accept whatever circumstance comes our way—as if we chose it—then we can be emotionally prepared. To be prepared emotionally is to visualize ourselves beforehand getting those feelings of doubts and nervousness, amid the pressure, and overcoming them.

Captain Sullenberger developed a presence over years of training for crisis situations that enabled him to respond with poise under pressure. "I think, in many ways, as it turned out, my entire life up to that moment had been a preparation to handle that particular moment," he said. Sully's beliefs and mental preparation coincided with the crisis presented to him, and as a result, he saved 155 lives.

At a recent golf tournament, a client of mine, Kyla I., was faced with unforeseen weather conditions. Hail mixed with snow and driving winds made most of the golfers miserable. Remember that to connect with your performance, anything that happens, that you can't control, is how it's supposed to be. When something unexpected such as crazy weather happens, it catches most people off guard, and their Trickster/Critic/Monkey Mind minds kick in. Your mind-set may be completely different, however, because you have worked on controlling your state. You tell yourself, "This is perfect. I wouldn't have it any other way." You act as if you chose the "bad" weather. The adversity inspires you. That's what the greatest have learned to do, to see adversity as a challenge and not a setback. When everyone else was complaining and wondering if and when the tournament would be canceled, Kyla stayed present, with no desires for more clement weather. She won the tournament.

Dr. Curt Tribble, head cardiac surgeon at the University of Virginia School of Medicine, brought in a resident physician in a life-

and-death operation, and the patient seemed to be slipping away. The resident, however, had prepared himself for such a situation. Dr. Tribble explains:

> The resident performed a highly unorthodox procedure in order to get air to the patient. The attending anesthesiologist said, "Wow, have you ever done that before?" The resident with absolute honesty, and not even a hint of sarcasm, looked at him and said, "No, but I've thought about it a lot."

In other words, the resident had dreamed of various situations that could come up and saw himself performing with poise under pressure. The best among us never stop dreaming or imagining new and more intense pressure situations and the solutions we'd manufacture. We must be prepared to roll with "bad" calls from the umpire, turbulent weather, nervousness, fear, anxiety—anything. To do this, we need equilibrium—a clear mind—one with no expectations of how things should be, and one that daydreams of contingencies, as exemplified by Charles Sullenberger and Dr. Tribble's resident physician.

Visualization: Creating a Consciousness of Success Under Pressure

Every noteworthy achievement started as an image in someone's mind. Excellence is within you, waiting to be accessed. Artists begin with an image in their minds, gold medalists see themselves winning the medal before they do, businesspeople see themselves getting the major account before it actually happens. Visualization is remembering or creating a picture in your mind—and the associated feelings—in order to create the state you want.

It starts with clarity, breaking from the endless stream of thoughts that weigh on you every day. When you have a clear mind and an unburdened heart (the product of a purpose that overrides circumstance), ideas will come; scenes emerge in your mind that relate to your goals and dreams. There's a constant battle between clutter and clarity in which images compete for a prime spot in your mind. When clarity and clear images of your goal dominate, possibilities open up.

As you learn to continually control your state and keep your primary goals in your consciousness, you can move toward those powerful images. In Lewis Pugh's attempt to do what many experts said was humanly impossible, he had to override logic and rational thinking. His coach, Tim Noakes, told CNN, "The moment you dive into cold water, your temperature drops and the brain sends a message to get out of the water. The first thing Lewis has to do is control that response." Pugh spent four hours a day visualizing, along with one hour a day swimming in cold water. He visualized his swim from beginning to end. "I can taste salt water in my mouth. I can hear the sounds of the engines, of Tim Noakes screaming at me. I can feel ice burning my skin; I can smell the sea air. I absolutely live that moment. I have swum the north pole hundreds of times in my mind," he told CNN.

No matter what business you're in, the ability to still your mind and imagine your future is paramount. Everything happens twice: first in your mind and then in your life. The results you're getting are directly tied to the images in your mind, the beliefs you have about those images, and your ability to connect with images of successful outcomes and feelings. What are the pressure moments in your day and in your business? Are you subjected to an overbearing boss or perhaps an extremely competitive job market? Whether you're try-ing to make a team, run a thriving business in a slow economy, or simply get a good job, it all is affected by your ability to see your day unfold in your mind the way you want, before it starts. If you can see the stressful events in your mind before they happen, and can then imagine your own confident response, you'll give yourself the best chance of staying focused and confident when the time comes.

Visualization is done to connect with a feeling in order to cre-ate the consciousness you desire. When you can visualize the pres-sure moments and can get the feeling of peace and confidence, even a fleeting tingling feeling of excitement, then you are reassociating your beliefs as they relate to your goal. Remember that beliefs can be expanded by repeated feelings of achieving your goal or becoming the person you want to become. You can get those feelings when you see, feel, hear, taste, and smell that image in your mind.

Here are a few visualization techniques to help you get those feelings and develop a consciousness of success under pressure:

- **Preview.** Visualize the events and circumstances of your upcoming performance. Use all your senses to imagine how it will feel. This is what many professional athletes, singers, and dancers do the night before a big game or performance. They see themselves performing well, doing the things they know they will be called on to do. You can do the same thing before a negotiation, meeting, or presentation.

- **Recall.** Remember an amazing performance. If you're an ath-lete, recall your best performance. If you're a musician, relive hitting the notes perfectly. If you're a salesperson, go back in time to a successful pitch to a challenging prospect.

◆ **Scene of success.** This visualization captures the scene immediately following a great moment. For example, you've just given an incredible presentation or gotten the game-winning hit: what happens in the twenty seconds after that? Visualize that scenario—how the audience responds, how your teammates or coworkers react, what you say and do, and so forth.

◆ **Relax.** There are two types of relaxation visualization. One is relaxing as a way to clear the mind (for example, imagining a peaceful nature scene), and the other is seeing yourself relaxed in pressure situations. (Note that relaxing under pressure means finding your ideal performance state for you and what you're doing; a Navy Seal relaxed under fire may have a different state of relaxation from that of an author with a deadline.)

◆ **Reframe.** If you are plagued by the memory of a mistake, you can change the memory in order to diminish the negative residual effects. Replay the event in your mind, seeing it the way you wanted it to go. (Refer to Chapter 5 for the reframing sequence.)

◆ **Mentors.** In this visualization, you imagine that people you highly respect—these can include industry leaders, coaches, even parents—are encouraging and inspiring you and your work or performance.

Before I write, I use a mentors visualization. I see myself entering an exclusive, ivy-covered building. I nod to the guard, a U.S. marine, who escorts me to my office, where I know that six or seven people are waiting for me. As we make our way to the office, the marine, in full uniform, walks purposefully and, in his professional manner, says how much he respects me and that it's an honor to escort me each day. I arrive in this beautiful office with vaulted ceilings and walls lined with brilliant books. In the center of the room is a table around which are seated Martin Luther King Jr., John Wooden (legendary basketball coach), Mike Krzyzewski (Duke basketball coach), Nelson Mandela, and a few other leaders I respect immensely. They are discussing the concepts in this book. The marine pulls my chair out for me, I thank him, and the people around the table take turns asking my opinion on various issues they're facing regarding focus, poise, leadership, and other subjects. After a few minutes of this, they get up to leave and all give me a hug or handshake and their blessing.

I have a song that I listen to as I'm walking down the hallway each time that anchors the visualization. This exercise forms a connection with the writing that helps me start each day with a clear mind, poised and ready to create.

Inherent in every pressure situation is the possibility of failure, and that's a good thing. Pressure gives us the opportunity for growth and extraordinary experiences, which is the core of a courageous life. In our affluenza culture of instant gratification, we tend to lose perspective on what gives meaning to life. When we seek mastery, however, we are preparing ourselves for a life of growth and learning that sets the stage for resonance, adversity and all. We can then transcend our day-to-day circumstances and the need to beat our opponents and instead focus on being our best selves. We thereby forge a connection with the performance, which provides incredible experiences. We win more often and are prepared for the unexpected. In crisis, danger becomes opportunity.

Key Points from Chapter 8

- Poise is a learned ability, one in which the performer becomes united with the task, vividly experiencing the moment.
- Poise is a reflection of balance and equilibrium; a clear mind and an unburdened heart.
- Four conditions pave the way for poise under pressure: clear perspective, mastery orientation, positive rivalry, and connection with the performance.
- When you feel resonance, everything else fades away: the score, the outcome, and possibly even your opponent. The pressure becomes energy that propels you.
- Focusing on connecting with your performance and fully experiencing the event is crucial to achieving resonance.
- Embracing your opponent as a vital component of your growth and experience can elevate your focus.
- Three elements largely affect connection with the performance: physiology, emotional preparation, and visualization.

Follow-Up Questions and Activities

- When have you felt the balance and focus of resonance in a performance? What kind of habits and routines can help you repeat that experience?
- What prevents you from getting that feeling?
- How can you incorporate the three mastery concepts of self-discipline, self-awareness, and personal growth into your daily life?

- Consider your rivals. Visualize them as components of your success rather than opponents who restrict it. How does that reappraisal affect your ability to be present and focused?
- Visualize your next performance. Feel the pressure and the nervousness that usually accompany it. See unexpected events happening and the chaos that may ensue. Immerse yourself in that feeling, and then get centered and relaxed in the pressure. See yourself coming through with poise and confidence.
- Pick a group of mentors and visualize them sitting around a table in your ideal office, encouraging and inspiring you.

Zoë and the Mind-Set for Growth

The Underlying Process of High Performance

He's not going to make it. He's not comfortable being uncomfortable.

—**Lou Piniella, Major League Baseball manager, speaking about a rookie's frustration with failure at Spring Training**

He has been called the most feared athlete in Olympic history. Greco-Roman wrestler Alexander Karelin never lost a match in thirteen years and did not give up a single point for six straight years. Karelin won gold medals at the '88, '92, and '96 Olympic Games. His conditioning, agility, and unmatched physical strength—he once carried a full-size refrigerator up eight flights of stairs—led him to be known as "the Experiment." When asked why he thought he was called that, Karelin said that others don't understand because, "I train every day of my life as they have never trained a day in theirs."

Olympic swimmer Ian Crocker, pushing his body intensely day after day, would often ask himself why he swims, as he approached his breaking point. At the Olympic level, training is a 365-day-a-year event, in the weight room, in the pool, and in the mind. The mental and physical battle can be incredibly draining: Ian took antidepressants after winning his first Olympic gold medal in 2000. Now he has a new outlook. Mostly, it seems, he swims to grow as a person, to learn and experience new things.

"After the Olympics," Crocker said, "the only questions you get asked by people are about the results. 'Did you win?' That can be a really difficult thing because there's so much more to it. I think the deeper part of the experience can get lost pretty easily. That was definitely one of my struggles after Athens." Crocker learned, perhaps, that the pursuit of a medal (he has four Olympic medals) can often lead to missing out on the journey. "Sometimes," he said, "the only reasons I can find to get out of bed in the morning to go work out is that my swimming career offers me a learning experience that I can't get anywhere else."

When Dr. Mimi Silbert started the Delancey Street Foundation, her purpose was not to win awards in business, which she did, but to turn around the lives of the people she worked with. To this end, she directed her efforts to teaching life skills. Silbert's fundamentals of success at Delancey are based on hard work, caring relationships, and a total-life educational model. She has a rare ability to develop people, and those people have achieved extraordinary success.

Extraordinary performers who perform at peak levels under pressure and live balanced, fulfilling lives seem to have a few "special talents." The first talent is the intense drive to improve. There is no substitute for hard work. The second talent is being an excellent learner. Practice does not make perfect. Knowing what to practice, what to learn, and how to learn are just as essential as hard work. The third talent, similar to the second, is a growth mind-set, which we will explore in this chapter.

An extraordinary performer with a fulfilling life is focused on the journey, not the destination, and if we listen closely and see clearly during that journey, life teaches us lessons on how to grow and improve. If we can abandon our self-consciousness and our attachment to the past and future, we can do extraordinary things and live greatly. The mind-set for growth is the pursuit of a powerful inner world that's unattached to the external goals we set (even as we pursue them intensely). This mind-set has a lively curiosity to search out possibilities of a life continuously expanding. In these pages we will become familiar with five core concepts for growth:

- Developing your sense of self
- Challenging what you know
- Failing valiantly
- Mastering the in-between moments
- Not taking things personally

Remember that in your pursuit of absolute fullness of life, more than building a career, you are building a life. Winning the gold medal is extremely costly if you're taking antidepressants in order to do it. Being the best at your job is meaningless if getting there requires that you sacrifice your family. You must keep your eyes on the ultimate goal: absolute fullness of life, represented by great experiences, great relationships, and the inner peace that comes from being one's true self.

In order to grow toward Zoë, we must be good learners, and to be good learners, we must not be attached to the outcome of what we do. We can never truly be great learners when we are reacting emotionally to every circumstance. The most important thing in growth and seeking extraordinary experiences is our inner world, not outer circumstances. We must learn to overcome the Critic, which is attached to our circumstances; to do this takes a strong sense of self.

 ## Growth Concept Number One: Develop Your Sense of Self

A person with a strong sense of self is less threatened by a failed outcome or being wrong. Strong people have no need to defend themselves, because they don't have the need to prove they're right. They've mastered the ego in order to learn and grow. This, of course, is very difficult when you're surrounded by the affluenza virus every day and the insecurity that accompanies it. When your sense of self is not determined by what you have, what you've done, or how others see you, then you have the fullest opportunity to grow and develop an identity that's empowering and far more secure.

A strong sense of self is one that's not tied to performance. As a professional baseball player in the Chicago Cubs organization, I lived in envy of those who performed better than I did. My personal value fell with each failure. It's an unstable confidence that arises only from successful outcomes. There should be something more that provides self-confidence, because as you improve and take on more challenges, you will fail more often.

Your sense of self is stronger when it finds its security in something other than the tangible symbols of success. Where, then, should security originate? It should come from the values emanating from your true self. Your true self lives to love, learn, and grow.

It seeks to use your gifts to serve the world. If what you do doesn't make a difference in anyone's life but yours, your sense of self does not increase. The more you help others, the better you feel about yourself and the easier it is to learn from failure, see opportunities, and grow toward Zoë.

A strong sense of self is connected to self-acceptance. Self-acceptance is increased by an expanded vision. That's one reason why international travel is a powerful experience. Going to a foreign country creates a certain level of discomfort; it places you in a position of unfamiliarity. Human nature wants to reject the unfamiliar, which is why change is so unsettling. When you travel abroad, you discover new ways of looking at things, find alternate ways of doing things, and live in constant awareness of things around you. We learn how people see us and the culture we're from, which in turn teaches us about ourselves. The increased self-awareness bolsters self-acceptance. Much of the problem of self-rejection is not that we dislike ourselves but that we don't know ourselves, or perhaps have buried our true selves.

Self-acceptance grows every time we choose integrity over popularity. To make a habit out of choosing integrity, it helps to have a strong support system. That doesn't mean you need your immediate family to support you, although it certainly is a bonus; it means selflessly loving and supporting others in order to connect with those who will support you. It can be a mentor, a neighbor, or even a Facebook "friend" you haven't seen in years. Someone who helps you be true to yourself is a valuable boost to a strong sense of self.

As you make the integrity choice more often, you'll more readily take responsibility for everything that happens in your life. Taking responsibility for the failures—the poor performances, the mistakes, the foolish deeds—is not easy or enjoyable, but it increases self-acceptance.

In order to truly grow, we must take risks, and to take risks, we must overcome the barrier of self-consciousness and attachment to the outcome that is afraid of failure. To do this, we need a strong sense of self, which will give us the courage and daring necessary to really step out onto that lonely ledge that puts integrity over popularity. A strong sense of self does not need to control others, nor does it need to control what happens to us. It simply lives with the knowledge that who we are, and who we are becoming, determines the quality of life we will lead and the legacy we will leave.

 ## Growth Concept Number Two: Challenge What You Know

The pursuit of growth is a journey of continually finding new ways to learn, develop self-mastery, and be fully present. It's a quest of learning how and what to learn. In other words, growth, especially toward Zoë, is the pursuit of wisdom.

Wisdom teaches us how to live and pursue fullness of life. In a way, wisdom is very personal, because no one has had the same experiences and lessons you've had, and thus, no one has the same wisdom as you. On the other hand, wisdom is very communal, because everyone else has wisdom that you do not. Wisdom is the pursuit of integrity, which is the state of being whole. To be whole is in part to connect with the wisdom and love of others, thus expanding our own love and wisdom. Wisdom sees the interconnectedness of life and how little of it our self-centeredness takes in.

We've all developed habits of seeing things a certain way, things we know to be true—only to change our opinions about these truths down the road as we learn new truths. The world was flat years ago; this was a fact until someone challenged what they knew.

The only way to grow is to accept that there is much to learn. To seek wisdom is to never stop questioning how things are done, what your beliefs are, and how you can live your dreams and help others live theirs. Perhaps the central question to study is how you can be fully present in this moment—what stops you and what helps you. When you're fully present, you have the most fruitful opportunity to grow, because in those moments you have no self-consciousness and no attachments to the past or the future.

You can challenge what you know by asking questions, paying attention, and listening closely. Be willing to change what you know if sufficient data back it up. Read informative books. Take off your self-conscious blinders. Seek counsel. Listen, look, and feel.

The things we know are the result of our habits of thinking. The brain, in its pattern-seeking ways, continually reinforces thoughts that, after a while, we accept as completely true, never to change. The way we talk to ourselves produces self-fulfilling prophecies. We struggle because we say we are struggling. We lose the promotion because we say we rarely get promoted.

Here are a few examples of ingrained habits of thinking that you may want to challenge:

- I have to _____ [get this promotion, win this event, do this thing].

Really? How do you know that getting this promotion, winning this event, or doing this thing is really the best course for you?

- I will be happier with more _____ or when I get _____ .

  This is the human facade. The grass is always greener; more always seems better. Getting more creates desire for more that never ends.

- I'm not able to _____ [achieve this goal, get this promotion, win this event].

  There are always logical reasons why you cannot do something. There are also reasons, perhaps a bit more imaginative, why you can.

- I'm struggling with _____ [whatever skill or task has been problematic for you].

  You're actually not struggling with anything right now except perhaps reading this sentence. When you talk in the present tense about what you've been struggling with, you're projecting the same for tomorrow.

- I always _____ [screw this up, lose to this person, fail in this situation].

  The fact that you've come up short in this exact situation many times in the past does not mean you will do so again. It means only that the Trickster will remind you of those failures and predict future failure for you. Callista B., from Chapter 6, failed nine straight times and then defeated the same opponent the tenth time, when it mattered most. You can do the same.

- I don't deserve to _____ [get a promotion, be truly loved, win a championship].

  The pursuit of excellence is deserving in and of itself. The combination of love, wisdom, and courage attracts abundance. Expect it.

You can challenge these and similar habits of thinking by first analyzing any such thoughts without judgment. Notice the patterns that appear. We generally have a handful of categories that we think about given spare time, and often those thoughts are limiting. You may counter, "I continually think this way because it's the way things are. I truly cannot do X [or, "I always do Y"]." When you argue for your limitations, as motivational speaker Les Brown says, you get to keep them. So, first, notice the internal monologue and whether those thoughts are empowering or limiting. Then learn to dismiss or replace the limiting thoughts, as outlined in Chapter 5.

We mere mortals were definitely sure at one point that humans could not fly (especially to the moon), could not run a mile in less than four minutes, and could not play in the NBA if they're five feet three inches tall, and that a group of convicted felons, almost all of whom were also drug addicts, could not run award-winning companies.

Those are things we knew to be true, and now we know otherwise. Our lives are always limited by our imagination and our readiness to challenge what we know. Keep dreaming. Take risks. Fail valiantly.

Growth Concept Number Three: Fail Valiantly

Growth, by definition, is expansion, becoming more than before. To grow, we must make decisions today that will result in risks taken tomorrow. We must learn how to be comfortable being uncomfortable and be willing to look foolish. We must fail.

In a win-at-all-costs culture, failing is not a popular concept. It is, however, an integral part of growth. We must embrace failure and get comfortable with it, as legendary baseball coach Skip Bertman said. When you're comfortable with failure, you can learn from it and won't fear it.

When we embrace failure, we can grow. When failure gets us down or angry, we may miss the learning. We all get upset when things don't go our way, but what counts is what we do after we're upset. Almost every great scientific discovery was at first derided as foolish or ludicrous, before it was accepted and applauded. An abundant life is one with a lot of failure, because there is no greatness without adversity, and there is no growth without failure.

Perhaps the question is not, do we need to fail in order to learn? What may be more relevant to ask is, how can we fail *and* learn? What do we need to do in order to see undesired outcomes as feedback and not failure? The stronger the sense of self, the less inclined we are to put our security in unstable things, and the more we'll be able to see failure as a

> I've missed more than nine thousand shots in my career. I've lost almost three hundred games. Twenty-six times, I've been trusted to take the game-winning shot and missed. I've failed over and over and over again in my life. And that is why I succeed.
>
> —**Michael Jordan**

potential opportunity for feedback and not a personal blow to the identity.

In writing, for example, the first draft is frequently garbage. It can be extremely trying for a writer to compose the first draft because so often it really stinks, but we need that garbage to provoke new ideas that lead to the final product.

In his book *Zen Mind, Beginner's Mind*, Shunryu Suzuki shares the following lesson:

> In our scriptures, it is said that there are four kinds of horses: excellent ones, good ones, poor ones, and bad ones. The best horse will run slow and fast, right and left, at the driver's will, before it sees the shadow of the whip; the second best will run as well as the first one, just before the whip reaches the skin; the third one will run when it feels pain on its body; the fourth will run after the pain penetrates to the marrow of its bones. You can imagine how difficult it is for the fourth one to learn to run. When we hear this story, almost all of us want to be the best horse. If it is impossible to be the best one, we want to be the second best. But this is a mistake. When you learn too easily, you're tempted not to work hard, not to penetrate to the marrow of a practice.
>
> If you study calligraphy, you will find that those who are not so clever usually become the best calligraphers. Those who are very clever with their hands often encounter great difficulty after they have reached a certain stage. This is also true in art, and in life.

When we win, we are like the best horse. There's no sting of the whip. This is a very dangerous position, a position where it's tempting to slack off. Victory is always dangerous, because it puts us in a place of potential pride and arrogance that ignores our shortcomings. Failure is just as dangerous, because we are inclined to internalize the failure and feel bad about ourselves. The route of a champion is very narrow, and few know the path. It's the path of risk, failure, learning, and growth.

Growth Concept Number Four: Master the In-Between Moments

The average round of golf takes approximately four hours and fifteen minutes to complete. During those four-plus hours, actual time playing the ball is perhaps five to ten minutes. The average length of a Major League Baseball game is approximately two hours and forty-five minutes, with the actual time spent with the ball in play also less than ten minutes. What about the other two hours and thirty-five minutes? It's easy to get caught up in the action and forget the moments in between. Business can be the same way, continually focusing on the next moment that will generate income. When we stare at the bottom line, we tend to lose sight of all that contributes to it. In our culture, often the only thing that matters is the goal and the outcome. The only thing that matters in Zoë is your internal world; everything else is a product of this. In the pursuit of Zoë, we are pursuing extraordinary experiences, from which extraordinary performances derive. If your experiences are what matters, then every moment is just as important as the next. The first day of spring training is just as important as the seventh game of the World Series.

You may say, no, the seventh game is more important, because the winners will make a lot more money, get a lot more fame, and have a better experience than the losers. So, that day is a more important day. It puts food on the table. You could say the same for any event, that the actual event is more important than the training that leads up to it.

What, then, is the difference between the person who wins the national championship and the one who loses? The next day, they are the same people with the same faults, the same fears, and the same person staring back in the mirror. The difference is that one of them will have more status, perhaps more money, and maybe more opportunities to get more of both. But is that what you really want? I believe, as you probably realize by now, that what you really want is not the money or status, but the feelings you'll get (or believe you'll get) from it. In other words, our day-to-day experiences are just as important as our performances, maybe even more so.

Here's how aikido master George Leonard puts it:

Our preoccupation with goals, results, and the quick fix has separated us from our own experiences. To put it more starkly, it has robbed us of countless hours of the time of our lives. We awaken in the morning and hurry to get dressed. (Getting dressed doesn't count.) We hurry to eat breakfast so that we can leave for work. (Eating breakfast doesn't count.) We hurry to get to work. (Getting to work doesn't count.) Maybe work will be interesting and satisfying and we won't have to simply endure it while waiting for lunchtime to come. And maybe lunch will bring a warm, intimate meeting, with fascinating conversation. But maybe not.

Once our basic needs are met (food, water, shelter, etc.), then increasing amounts of money and status provide less and less return, unlike the returns of love, wisdom, and courage, which yield endless joy, challenge, and fulfillment.

So, how do we master the in-between moments? In-between moments comprise the daily activities that need to be done and that we usually try to rush through to get to something important. Taking a shower, driving to work, standing in line, making photo-copies, washing the dishes—these are the in-between moments. So engrossed in our drive for more, we want to skip the majority of our life to get to what's important. If you really want to be an extraordi-nary performer and to have extraordinary moments, you'll learn to be more present in the moments in between.

To practice being fully present during the common moments of your day, consider nothing to be more important than the moment you're in. The desire to get through this moment, to be elsewhere, and the anxiety that comes when we must wait in line, sit in a meeting, or crawl through traffic are part of the daily challenge of mastery.

One of the essential components of mastery is to pay atten-tion, because there is a lesson in each moment, a teacher in every individual, and beauty always waiting. Mastery is a unique journey in that it exists only in the present. Nothing matters except right here, right now, and that is exactly why so few people are in tune with mastery. The Trickster, the Critic, and the Monkey Mind all endlessly jump to the past and the future, but real growth takes place only in the present moment. That's why mastery is essentially a goalless journey: the "goal" is always to master this moment, to accept it and be fully present with it, whatever it contains, whereas normally a goal is a future thing.

If we are to learn our life's lessons, we must be present, and then we must pay attention. Most of the time, lessons are so subtle that we miss them, perhaps quickly jumping over them in order to get to the "real" thing we were supposed to do or learn. Being present has its own lessons. One is the lesson of acceptance: what you resist will persist; what you accept will desist. Another is the lesson of beauty: it is always there, often blocked by our self-centered eyes, doubts, and fears. Third is the lesson of peace: we always have access to peace, if we trust and accept, and if we learn how to control our energy.

Louisiana State University swimmer Colleen B. learned the lesson of acceptance as she was stuck in rush-hour traffic. Like most of us, her first reaction was to resist the gridlock and become frustrated and anxious. As soon as she accepted the standstill and let go of her need to be out of the jam, she saw some beautiful bluebonnet flowers on the side of the road, which she would have missed had she been able to coast along at the speed limit. Seeing those flowers brought her the peace and energy of nature in her busy day, and she could feel her own energy returning.

When we are busy, we miss so much. When we rush through assignments that seem bureaucratic and pointless, we miss the details that give us the knowledge to make a difference later on. So often, we zip through life to get to the next event, the next item on the to-do list, the next achievement. All the while, life sits silently, patiently, waiting for us to notice what it's trying to tell us. Often it's trying to say, *slow down*. Slow down so you can sense beauty, so new ideas can come, so new relationships can build. You don't have to go to the Bahamas to think new, creative thoughts.

For many of us, stopping in contemplation is difficult because we're not ready to be alone with our thoughts. We would rather chase something, anything, than encounter solitude. One day, however, we may look in the mirror and for the first time truly see that person, the gifts that have been given, and the opportunities that await. Then we can take the next step in our quest to truly live. It takes time, however, where we're fully present, to penetrate to the marrow of life and see what's really there.

The moments in between, the times spent doing nothing "important," are no less important than the moment for which we're preparing. The ideal performance state is one of feeling rather than thinking. How do you get that effortlessness, heralded by a clear mind and an unburdened heart? You get it from all those moments in between. When you're busy hurrying to get to the important moments, all that time could be training for the most important moment of your life: the one right now.

The temptation in business is to dash from one appointment or task to the next, seeking high productivity. The best businesses, how-ever, are built on strong relationships, and strong relationships emerge when people are present with each other. The times between meet-ings and events are opportunities to harness your energy and develop the relationships that you bring to those "important" times. Whether it's a day full of meetings, or even a day out golfing during which you restrain yourself from rushing between holes, if you are fully present during the moments in between, regardless of how you perform, you will give yourself the best chance of creating consistency.

 ## Growth Concept Number Five: Don't Take Things Personally

A powerful mind-set is one that values the benefits of growth so highly that it's willing to endure the possible embarrassment of looking foolish. Rarely do we have sustaining peace and clarity, because our constant view of ourselves as the center of our particular universe continually reminds us of our limits, weaknesses, and failures. So, we measure ourselves against others and live in this constant self-conscious state of comparison. We know we're not perfect, so our thoughts easily leapfrog to what other people are thinking about us.

Self-consciousness is a precursor of fear and tension as we think about the past and the future and of how we'll be viewed. The surest way to overcome self-consciousness is, as you've been told many times by now, through love, wisdom, and courage. Love, by definition, focuses on others and how to serve the greater good, whereas self-consciousness is focused inward. Love dares to battle through your self-consciousness in order to bring to the world the greatness that is within you. In your self-consciousness, nobody wins. In your rising above it, everyone benefits. Wisdom sees the expanded picture and not what may be wrong or offensive. Courage uses love to act despite our self-consciousness.

One way to overcome self-consciousness is to practice not taking things personally. In order to learn, we need to be objective; we can't let emotions cloud our focus. Getting caught up in what other people are thinking affects just about everything we do. How we dress, talk, act, and think are all affected by how we want others to see us and by how we think they see us.

Mired in our self-consciousness, we often have negative thoughts about others because we think they are thinking about us, probably something about how we fall short of expectations. The reality is that they are thinking about us far less than we assume, and wasting our thoughts on them severely limits our learning and growth. Even if someone is rude to you, chances are that the person is having a bad day, and you just stepped into it.

When you engage with someone who treats you poorly, it's hard not to attract that person's energy. Someone who is struggling is likely to speak negatively toward you, but you mustn't get caught up in it if your goals are important to you. When you do not take things personally, you are able to increase your sense of wonder and curiosity as you seek understanding and growth, unafraid of what people will say. To not take things personally, you must remove the threats, which come from the ego. Humility and gratitude help you do that.

Growth over Fear

Fear is the chief obstruction to performance, to extraordinary experience, and to the process of both, which is growth. We cannot keep our most precious dreams and goals in clear focus and respond effectively to setbacks when we are constantly on the defensive. We cannot be emotionally resilient when we continually feel threatened. The ego must be controlled in order for us to overcome the self-consciousness and attachments that stymie the self-mastery needed for us to grow and improve every day.

We've all had traumatic experiences sometime in our lives. Childhood is a time of learning, and sometimes we "learn" that the world is a dangerous place and that we need to protect ourselves in it. Addressing this subject, Elizabeth Kubler-Ross, author of *Life Lessons*, stated, "Even more challenging is to let go of defense mechanisms that helped us survive in childhood, because once these tools are no longer needed they can turn against us." Kubler-Ross was explaining that walls were built to help us at one point, but those walls might have stopped being useful and now actually hem us in.

Here are a few questions that will help you determine whether you are hiding behind the ego and its defenses:

+ Are you willing to be uncomfortable?
+ Are you willing to look foolish and laugh at your foolishness?
+ Are you willing to fail?
+ Do you need to be right?
+ Do you often take things personally or feel threatened?

Fear, the derivative of self-centeredness, blocks our path. Focusing on growth (toward Zoë) as the ultimate in self-actualization is a powerful way to overcome fear. Alexander Karelin, perhaps the best wrestler of all time, trained harder than anyone else. Ian Crocker swims to see what he can learn and how he can grow. Mimi Silbert runs her foundation in order to develop people (and not the other way around). Each of them provides us with a lesson in how to pursue fullness of life and to subsequently achieve extraordinary success.

Key Points from Chapter 9

+ Every day is no more or less important than the next when you focus on growth.
+ In order to grow, we must be good learners; to be good learners, we must not be attached to the outcome of what we do.

- We must learn to overcome the Critic, attached to our circumstances; to do this takes a strong sense of self.
- A strong sense of self is powered by a purpose beyond the self. Attachment comes from allowing the ego to override purpose.
- The moments in between our tasks and goals are perhaps the most important moments of our lives.
- We must get comfortable with failure in order to learn from it.
- The less we take things personally, the more we can grow.

Follow-Up Questions and Activities

- Consider that everything that happens, every circumstance, is here to help you or teach you. What are the lessons life is teaching you today?
- Acknowledge that everyone you come across this week may be your teacher. A two-year-old may teach you patience. A seventy-two-year-old may teach you wisdom. A panhandler may teach you gratitude. Others may teach you what not to do. Who is your teacher today? Were there any potential teachers you brushed off recently?
- Contemplate the following idea: The messenger will continue to send the message until the message is delivered. Are there any messages that you're not getting? Consider things that repeat in your life as unlearned lessons, like a message in a bottle, that you're supposed to stop and contemplate.
- Have you failed yet today? Why not? What risks have you not taken that are holding you back because of your self-consciousness?
- What beliefs that you knew to be true before are no longer true for you now? Are there possibly more?

- Observe your self-talk. Is it empowering or limiting? What are you reinforcing with your repeated thoughts?
- When you take your next shower, try to be fully present, with no thoughts of anything but getting clean and relaxing. Note in what way this act interrupts the stream of thoughts of your day, as well as what that leads to.

Maslow, Michael Jordan, and the Navy Seals

Three Hallmarks of Extraordinary Leaders

The difference between champions and near champions is the ability to play for something outside of self.

—Lou Holtz, Hall of Fame football coach

Jim Tressel, head football coach at Ohio State University, took a trip to the little town of Gambier, Ohio. He went to speak with Jim Steen, Kenyon College swim coach. Tressel, who has guided the Buckeyes to five Big Ten championships in eight seasons, sought out Steen, who has won forty-nine national championships (yes, forty-nine). Tressel and Steen have both learned a few things over the years, including how to develop leaders, how to focus on the process of high performance, and, perhaps most of all, how to build a family.

Phil Jackson became head coach of the Chicago Bulls in 1989 and inherited the best basketball player in the world. Michael Jordan was great, but the team was not. Jackson instilled the values of compassion and selflessness in a league of egos and false bravado. The Bulls went on to win six NBA championships, and Jackson won four more with the Los Angeles Lakers (through 2009). Jackson, Tressel, and Steen are powerful coaches because they are good leaders.

> It has always been my philosophy, and I really believe this sincerely, that a football player is a person first, a tennis player is a person first, a swimmer is a person first. Then you go ahead and coach the activity that he's participating in.
>
> —Dick Vermeil, NFL football coach

The best leaders see what's possible for the group and empower the group members to reach that level. They know the details of performance extremely well and communicate those details in a way that inspires. Inspiration comes from teaching—great leaders are great teachers. They use their sport or work to convey new ways of seeing the world; what's possible, and how to live more fully, love more deeply, and experience life in ways that promote learning and growth. When people have an inspiring vision for the future and are given tools to learn and grow, they will do whatever tasks they face with a higher level of proficiency, as well as with incredible loyalty.

Leadership is the development of people, influencing them to connect with a vision beyond themselves. Groups and teams whose members work together, pushing and motivating each other to constantly improve, have a unique culture, created from the top. There are certain other things leaders do, beyond the areas of technical expertise and disciplined practice, that make all the difference in the world. In my experience, three habits stand out in the lives and teaching of the greatest coaches and leaders. These men and women all do the following:

- Redefine success
- Connect individuals with a vision beyond themselves
- Seek self-mastery—and help others do the same

The best leaders create a culture that develops people to live fully, experience vividly, and have fun along the way. Through the daily message of their own lives, they set the tone, because they live what they teach. Whether it is teaching athletes or executives, in the field of baseball or business, the basic principles of extraordinary performance are the same. It starts with a leader who, far beyond the Xs and Os of strategy and tactics, studies how to empower and enrich the lives of those he or she leads.

Redefine Success

Hall of Fame basketball coach John Wooden won ten national championships at UCLA, including seven in a row. He defined success as "peace of mind, which is a direct result of self-satisfaction in knowing you made the effort to become the best of which you are capable." Jim Tressel slightly adjusts Wooden's definition for his Buckeyes: "Success is the inner satisfaction and peace of mind that comes from knowing you did the best you were capable of *for the group*."

In our culture, success is often measured by what you have, what you've done, and how you compare with others. In Wooden's and Tressel's definitions, those three are never mentioned. The best coaches set goals and then focus intensely on the process of achieving those goals. But it doesn't stop there. They pursue success that goes beyond their goal of a championship and the temporary rewards it brings.

Tressel's definition of success focuses on inner satisfaction, peace of mind, and doing your best—for the group. "[Tressel] builds his program around first, morals as a team and as a man, second, closeness, and then football," said Malcolm Jenkins, one of Tressel's all-Americans. You might summarize Tressel's definition as having a powerful spirit (inner satisfaction and peace), giving it your best shot (the best you were capable of), and having a purpose beyond yourself (for the group).

Frosty Westering, four-time national champion football coach, focused on the development and growth of his athletes as people, first and foremost. According to *Sports Illustrated*, for Westering, "conventional measures of success are unimportant." The article continues, "Winning, he says with neither irony nor embarrassment, is 'a by-product of learning to live decently.' In fact Westering is less interested in football than he is in 'shaping players' lives and influencing their hearts and minds.'"

Before a big game, one of Frosty's players stood up and said, "They're here to *beat* us; we're here to *be* us." His teams were dominating because his players learned that fullness of life was pursued by being their true selves and serving others. They learned to love and respect each other, as well as their opponents, which created powerful energy that enabled them to perform their best.

John Wooden didn't scout opposing teams. He did not care to know what anyone else was doing. This allowed him, I believe, to be innovative and focused on development. He was determined to make his team the best it could be, regardless of how they compared to others. You may say, "That's easy for him—he had the best talent."

But Wooden didn't recruit either. The talent came to him. His ability to develop people was a great draw. He was much more concerned with personal and team development than comparison to others. W. Chan Kim and Renee Mauborgne echoed the same idea in their best-selling book *Blue Ocean Strategy*: "The only way to beat the competition is to stop trying to beat the competition."

It's the biggest mistake teams and coaches make. They would do better to focus on the process of high performance, which is quite different. When you focus on defeating an opponent, you're focusing on something largely out of your control, which creates tension and easily takes you out of the present. (If it were completely in your control, it would be on your to-do list and not a goal.) In order to achieve the goal, we must stay fixed on the elements of the goal. Jim Collins, bestselling author of *Good to Great* and *Built to Last*, listed twelve myths regarding great companies. Myth number ten: "The most successful companies focus primarily on beating the competition." The reality, Collins says, is that "visionary companies focus primarily on beating themselves."

Or as I say it, the best teams and companies focus on being their *best selves*. To be your best self is to overcome your natural self-centeredness and the limits it imposes. Phil Jackson works on this with his teams by focusing on selflessness and compassion. These powerful virtues help silence the voice of the Trickster, the judgment of the Critic, and the endless chatter of the Monkey Mind. Rather than making "winning" or "profit" their ultimate goals, top organizations focus on using their sport or business to make a difference in the lives of their team members and the world we live in.

You may wonder about those organizations that seem to have no interest in the welfare of their members or of anyone else, for that matter, and still lead their industry. In the same category are

Defining Best

Frosty Westering, Pacific Lutheran University
football coach, four-time national champion

The question is, doesn't everyone want to be number one? Well, we all want to win, but it depends on how we define winning, and how we understand the joy of competing, without the fear of failure. Defining what *best* is, is a key thing. Society says we won four national championships, but we also lost four. But the ones that we lost were great games, just terrific games. What I've done is try to take the three definitions of *best* and lay them out in a way that our guys understand it. First is being *the best*. That's what everyone talks about. Being the NBA champion. When you win it, you're everything; when you don't, you go home a loser. I don't believe that at all, but that's something you've got to challenge. Being the best is a by-product of other things.

The second definition is being *your best*. Well, how do you know what your best really is? I think that's really the key in coaching— to try to help a person reach his or her potential, whatever that is. So, you ask, "How do you measure potential?" There's all these fitness tests that they run—speed, agility, things at the combine—but there's another one, the inner game, the inside test, which is even greater than these. You gotta be able to run, you gotta be able to hit and do all these other things, but the bottom line is, it isn't that that really makes the difference. Parents tell their kids to do their best, but so many times we aren't our best. We try hard, but we're not our best. So, we gotta figure out another way that you can deal with competing, and again understanding that we may not be the best, we may not be our best, but we can accomplish one thing, and that's the third definition . . . which is *your best shot.*

Your best shot is just preparing to do what you've gotta do and going out and loving doing it, even if you aren't doing very well. You love doing it because you've worked hard and you understand that that's what makes you better. And when you do that often enough, even when you're not doing it very well, and you're surrounded by others that believe that, you start bringing out the best in each other. That's what I call the double win.

The double win is bringing out the best in teammates and yourself. When you do that, even though you're not your best, they help you bring that out, because on a given day, you never know who it is that's gonna be right there. You learn to give it this best shot in everything you do, even when it isn't very good. So, then you take a look at how that relates to being the best. By giving it your best shot all the time and loving to compete, you start doing your best more of the time, and you become the best more often.

superstar athletes who only look out for number one. First off, we're seeking absolute fullness of life, of which the banners and awards are the by-product. Second, if your talent (or money) is far in excess of everyone else's, you may be able to get away with a lot more than others. In the end, however, life always has a way of evening things out. Consider the New York Yankees and New York Mets of the past few years, who tower over the rest of baseball in financial resources but struggle to reach their potential. It's more often the case that if you have the affluenza virus, your joy and passion will be replaced by tension and anxiety, and your performance will suffer.

When we practice selflessness and nonjudgmental awareness, in the manner of Phil Jackson, we can begin to see the larger purpose, beyond winning a game, making a lot of money, or achieving a certain status. "With the Bulls I've learned that the most effective way to forge a winning team is to call on the players' need to connect with something larger than themselves," Jackson said. "Even for those who don't consider themselves 'spiritual' in a conventional sense, creating a successful team—whether it's an NBA champion or a record-setting sales force—is essentially a spiritual act. It requires the individuals involved to surrender their self-interest for the greater good so that the whole adds up to more than the sum of the parts."

> Find a place within yourself where success and failure don't matter, a place where you can engage in battle without compromise.
>
> —Jim Steen, Kenyon College swim coach

We all have a deep need, I believe, to be a part of something beyond profits and losses, winning and losing. Many of us go through life and never connect with that need, constantly trying to fill that longing with more wins, more money, more promotions. Tension and anxiety ensue, because we never have true freedom in performance when we are dependent on the outcome to fill our deep needs.

In *The Power of Story*, Jim Loehr describes an offer he makes to people who attend his workshops. His office is in one of two towers 175 feet high, 36 feet apart. He offers anyone five million dollars to walk across a twelve-inch-wide plank between the two towers. The plank has a bit of give to it, and the winds can get strong up there. Chance of success: 80 percent. Would you do it? Would you risk your life for a pile of money if there were statistically a 20 percent chance of death? What if it were fifty million dollars? Loehr got few takers, even at fifty million. But then he asks another question: "What if your family was on the other side and you had to cross the plank to save their lives?" For many people, that is a purpose for which they would risk life and limb.

Perhaps the best gift you could give your family is a person who seeks love, wisdom, and courage above all else. As you grow in mind, body, and spirit, your energy cannot help but transfer to those around you. Together you'll find a collective purpose that's worth sacrificing for.

Whether in reference to family, friends, teammates, or anyone else, when the central purpose of your life revolves around serving others, a powerful series of events begins to unfold. Fear loses some of its grip, since fear is inward focused, while service is by its nature focused on others. You develop relationships that carry you in the tough times. Your life becomes more meaningful, which promotes the inner peace needed to grow and have great experiences.

Great organizations have a servant-oriented focus. Jim Collins's research on visionary companies reveals a recurring theme: they focus on making a contribution to society, with profits as the by-product. In other words, their definition

> Goals are important but it's important to understand that people are not defined by their goals and whether or not they reach them. A win or a loss does not make you or me a better person. We have to separate who we are from what we do . . . it's vital to distinguish between purpose and goals. Understanding the difference between purpose and goals is essential to understanding the true definition of success.
>
> **—Jim Tressel, head football coach, Ohio State University**

of success revolves around a powerful purpose, and that purpose is to make a difference in people's lives.

A clear and meaningful purpose allows us to be more present in our performance because we become less attached to the outcome of our goals. Dawn Staley and the many other Olympians who experience vividly and live fully are stellar examples: they play to win, but winning is not the reason they play.

 ## Connect Individuals with a Vision Beyond Themselves

When Lewis Pugh set out to swim at the geographic north pole in only a Speedo, he was carried by a meaningful purpose. Success for him was doing his part to make a difference in the devastating effects of global warming. With this powerful purpose, he set out a vision of what he wanted to accomplish (swim one kilometer at the north pole), and his purpose guided him every day. The very real fears he faced each day were met with the strength of his purpose and the daily focus on his vision.

A vision beyond yourself is a goal that serves the greater good. A meaningful purpose—such as to make a difference in the lives of others—is more of a North Star, a directional guide, whereas a vision has a direct outcome. The purpose provides meaning and inspiration; the vision provides direction and focus.

Another group of people who regularly confront extreme danger and must come to terms with their fears are the Navy Seals (U.S. Navy Special Forces Unit). To become a Seal, you need to graduate from BUDS (Basic Underwater Demolition Seal training). BUDS is a six-month training program infamous for Hell Week, in which the majority of the enlistees drop out. During that five-day week, each potential Seal gets four hours of sleep total. The rest of the time they're being pushed to the limits, mentally, physically, and emotionally. When you've got a drill sergeant in your face, hosing you down with water as you're trying to eke out a few more push-ups, and everything within you wants to quit, there must be something deeper to prevent you from giving in to what your body so desperately wants to do. When I asked Navy Seal Jeff N. what got him through Hell Week, he said, "I focused on my team. I didn't want to let my team down. The other thing was that quitting was not an option. Nothing was going to stop me except my body literally breaking down."

> When a single blade of grass is cut, the whole world quivers.
>
> —**Author unknown**

In whatever vocation you have, there is the opportunity to face your fears, challenge your limits, and overcome doubt and anxiety. It doesn't matter if you drive a truck for a living or a Formula One racecar, if you're a CEO or a shoe salesman. No matter what you do during the day, assuming it doesn't completely go against your values, you can focus your energy in a way that creates an incredible presence. And if you can combine growth, love, and passion with your vocation, it's possible to reach a state of resonance so compelling that you would give your life for it.

The greatest leaders help us find that resonance. They help us choose what to think about and where to place our attention. They focus on connecting with each individual in order to help people feel positive about who they are, what's possible, and their significance to the big picture. Resonance is built on relationships, between your values and your actions, your mind and your heart, yourself and others, and yourself and the environment around you.

To be a great leader is to study and learn how to build those relationships to their full potential. Building a relationship with another person starts with a connection on some level. A strong bond starts by building rapport.

Rapport is based on empathy, which is a connection with what the other person is feeling. The best communicators understand that communication is mostly nonverbal and that everything you do and say communicates—you cannot "not communicate." According to one study, 7 percent of communication is the words you use, 38 percent is your tone of voice, and 55 percent is your posture and physiology. Dealers in Vegas, for example, are not allowed to stand with their arms crossed, because this is an uninviting posture. To gain rapport most effectively is to match the other person's posture and physiology, tone, and words, in a subtle way. It's called pacing, and it takes active listening to another level. (With active listening, the listener listens intently, occasionally repeating and/or summarizing what the other person is saying.)

If, for example, someone who reports to you is angrily pacing and talking loudly, sitting and speaking quietly would not put you in a position to match that person. If, however, you were to walk with him, match his volume, and actively listen to what he says, then you could eventually lead him to sit down, talk in a more relaxed manner, and go from there. First pace, then lead.

To really build a connection with someone is to connect with what the person really cares about. Say you're working with a new team or organization, and you want to build rapport on an individual basis. You meet with an employee and ask, "What is most important to you about your job?" She may respond, "I want to be challenged." (In my experience, we all want to be challenged in our lives, especially in what we're gifted at doing, so that we can be creative and grow.) Next you may ask her, "What does being challenged give you?" Perhaps she'll say, "It allows me to be creative and gives me a sense that I'm needed and useful." You may then ask, "What is important to you about being needed and useful?" Perhaps she'll say, "It gives me security." The idea is to continually ask what is important to her and what that gives her, until she expresses the root of what she really wants. Usually, when you hear either the same answer or an answer with nothing more beyond that comment, you've found the person's highest value in that area. The higher the value you can elicit (such as security, love, or peace), the more options you'll have to satisfy that need. In this example, now that you know security is important to this individual, you can connect the vision of the group and the purpose of the team with security.

> The pursuit of a single goal often inhibits the risk taking and creative thinking necessary for personal growth.
>
> —Jim Steen, Kenyon College swim coach

With larger groups, you may not be able to connect individually with each person on the team. If you're the leader, your goal is always to help those you lead continually see opportunities and ways to grow personally and professionally, while giving them a vision of what's possible in their lives and with the team. As the head of your division or head coach, you can't always visit with everyone, but you can develop a culture in which people sincerely connect with and support each other. If the culture of your organization is based on a meaningful purpose, a clear vision for the group, and self-mastery, then you've got a great chance of doing just that.

Seek Self-Mastery—and Help Others Do the Same

When Abraham Maslow studied the lives of extraordinary people—those who performed at extremely high levels *and* lived balanced, fulfilling lives—he found that they had an ability to experience fully and to live deeply. As we revisit Maslow's eight behaviors of self-actualization—total absorption in the experience, growth choices, self-awareness, honesty, intuition, self-development, peak experiences, and lack of ego defenses—we can see their relation to self-mastery. Self-mastery is self-awareness, self-education, and self-discipline. The pursuit of self-mastery is the quest for freedom, in which out of awareness, education, and discipline come growth and extraordinary experiences.

Mastery, as with wisdom, starts with reverence. Reverence comes from realizing that mastery awaits you, just as the best decision awaits every choice, the best move awaits every circumstance, and freedom awaits all of us. With mastery we make better decisions, act more wisely, and live more freely.

In reverence we become humble and grateful as our vision expands and we see all that's possible. Humility opens the door for learning and connecting with others. Through humility we find wisdom. The value of wisdom is far greater than knowledge, because while knowledge teaches us about life, wisdom teaches us how to live. Those who seek wisdom hold self-mastery as one of the highest aspirations, because mastery is not subject to one's moods and petty desires but to a strict longing for honor and integrity. Self-mastery reveals the greatness within you and the possibilities that await. It is a never-ending education in life.

In 2002, before the football season began, Jim Tressel flew down to the University of Miami to pick the brain of the reigning national champion head coach, Larry Coker. Tressel's Buckeyes ended up in the national championship game, against Coker's Hurricanes. The Buckeyes won in double overtime. Tressel knew he must keep learning or stop growing.

Self-mastery is a crucial pursuit in leadership, because in order to elevate the performance of the group, the leader must learn to humbly serve the members while maintaining his or her self-assuredness. Phil Jackson cites the book *The Tao of Leadership*: "The wise leader is of service: receptive, yielding, following. The group member's vibration dominates and leads, while the leader follows. But soon it is the member's consciousness that is transformed. It's the job of the leader to be aware of the group member's process; it is the need of the group member to be received and paid attention to. Both get what they need, if the leader has the wisdom to serve and follow."

A major part of serving the group is teaching personal development. The "goalless" quest of self-mastery is to learn self-control in order to grow, which is a process that never ends. You may ask why the concerted focus on growth when there is no end, but that's like asking why you should live when you know you will one day die. Growth *is* the end, or you could say that it is the meaning central to truly living.

Some of the best moments in life are the times when we're striving, learning, and growing; we're challenged in something at which we're talented, pursuing something meaningful. The games and practices, the presentations to coworkers and to major clients—all become the same: an opportunity to feel resonance. Michael Jordan was asked what he loved most about playing basketball, and he said he loved to practice, because in practice it was pure basketball. In practice he was challenged in what he was good at doing, he could connect with his teammates, and he could just be Mike. No crowds, no score, no frills. I believe he was able to perform masterfully under pressure because practices and games became one and the same for him—an opportunity to feel resonance.

Self-mastery strips away everything that's not us and gets us in tune with who we really are and how we want to feel. Pursuing self-mastery is seeking to be fully present and having both a clear mind and an unburdened heart. To maintain this presence 100 percent of the time is unrealistic, especially with our natural human tendencies to live in the past and future. Therefore, we need constant renewal.

In order to continue to grow, we must constantly renew our minds. The renewal process is a matter of quieting the mind in order to see things from a different perspective, overcoming our self-centered viewpoint, cultural bias, and prejudices. What does it mean to renew our minds? It means to continually rid ourselves of limited thinking, familiar ways of doing things, and everything else that's not our selves, to see the world with fresh eyes. To do this, we must regularly "reboot" our system of mental processing in order to eliminate the clutter. With the clutter gone, clarity comes, and with it, new ideas. Then we realize how little we know, and this realization facilitates a humble desire to learn more.

The best leaders, as with the best performers, have vast imaginations and regularly exercise their minds within the imagination. It's nearly impossible to be a great leader without regular renewal, because leadership involves constantly providing fresh ideas and motivation so that team members believe in themselves and each other. Thus, leaders must have the self-awareness to know when they're not present, when they need to get centered, and when their preoccupation with themselves is blocking their view of possibilities. Leaders must be able to see the group's success in their mind's eye as well as the path to get there—and then pass that vision on to the team.

Above all, a great leader serves the needs of the group. How? By knowing what the group needs and what it's going to take to get them where they need to go. The great leader connects with each person—or in larger groups with the key people—in such a way that everyone buys into the vision and serves each other in the process. The vision is most powerful when it's focused on something bigger than the individuals involved and when it helps each member grow as a person and as a unit.

The fundamental unit of a great team or company is a powerful individual. If that individual can overcome self-centeredness and redefine success in a way that has a powerful purpose, connect with a vision beyond the self, and seek self-mastery, then he or she can move toward absolute fullness of life.

Key Points from Chapter 10

- ◆ Leadership is the development of people, influencing them to connect with a vision beyond themselves.
- ◆ Great leaders do three things beyond the areas of technical expertise and disciplined practice: they redefine success, connect individuals with a vision beyond themselves, and seek and teach self-mastery and personal growth.
- ◆ Success in our culture is often measured by what you have, what you've done, and how you compare with others—but that's not how the best leaders measure success.

- The best coaches and leaders define success with a meaningful purpose, one that serves the greater good.
- Extraordinary organizations focus on being their best selves, not beating the competition.
- A powerful leader inspires individuals to connect with something bigger than themselves, helps each member grow as a person, and helps the members grow together as a unit.

Follow-Up Questions and Activities

- What is most important to you about what you do?

   Why do you want to _____ [win a championship, make more money, get that promotion]?

   What is important to you about that? What will that give you? Keep asking yourself what your answer will give you, until there is nothing more you want beyond that. That final answer is what you want, more than your tangible goal, and often there are different ways of getting it.
- What is the purpose in your work that gives meaning to what you do?
- How does your definition of success correlate with what you value most about work?
- What is the vision for your next major goal, and how does that relate to your purpose?
- In your pursuit of self-mastery, what do you need to do to increase your self-awareness, self-education, and self-discipline?
- What can you do today to renew your mind, to bring the ideas that will benefit tomorrow?

Conclusion
A New Way of Life

This time, like all times, is a very good one, if we but know what to do with it.

—Ralph Waldo Emerson

In our journey together thus far, we've seen the powerful influence of culture and how we're exposed every day to the affluenza virus. This inhibits our pursuit of what we really want: great experiences, great relationships, and the discipline and self-control that lead to a life of freedom and passion. We looked at how we get in our own way more than anything else and at how love, wisdom, and courage form the foundation for extraordinary performance and the powerful energy of resonance. We also saw how suffering and discipline are intertwined and how living in fear prevents us from truly living.

Armed with the knowledge of your self-centered nature and its limiting effects, you have the option each day to move away from fear and toward high performance and long-term fulfillment. You can choose to lead with the heart, expand our vision, and be fully present. To lead with the heart is to connect with your true self— that is, to seek who you are at your best and how that person would live, feel, and compete. To expand your vision is to continually adjust your map of the world to see the unseen: the ideas, beauty, and focus that redefine each moment. An expansive vision captures the wisdom that leads to learning, growth, and great experiences.

As you learn more, you'll challenge your old beliefs and pursue a purpose that serves the greater good. To be fully present is to have a clear mind and an unburdened heart as you connect with the beauty and excellence of each moment. For this you need to keep a simple mind and focus on what matters most—your internal world. It takes courage to live in the present because it's there that you see who you really are. This is where you connect with your true self, as well as the sacred moments of resonance.

Leading with your heart, expanding your vision, and being fully present creates a positive energy that leads to poise under pressure. You'll exhibit a new swagger, be more focused, be more relaxed, have more enjoyment, and be more disciplined than ever before. These five markers, which reveal (and enhance) your level of presence and poise, can be measured in each performance and in your life every day.

The pursuit of love, wisdom, and courage is a quest for self-mastery, in which the performance exists for the experience and in which your desires get molded more around developing a powerful spirit than external rewards. (The by-product, of course, *is* more external rewards.) You'll gain self-control and be more yourself as you remove the pride and ego that are constantly under threat. Your improved performances are a subset of great experiences, in which challenge, growth, and passion are leading you to a higher quality of life, far beyond that of the gold medal. Resonance is the reward, one unwritten about in magazines and newspapers but immeasurably valuable in your heart. It's the electric feeling of being fully present and congruent doing what you love.

One of my goals with this book has been to encourage you to live authentically and courageously, pursuing resonance and Zoë, beyond your external ambitions. Perhaps by now your ever-expanding vision has offered a glimpse of the incredible journey ahead—the one that compels you to be totally engaged, passionately involved in the moment in something you love. As more authentic moments begin to unfold, where nothing exists except the here and now and your mind, body, and spirit flow together as one, the elements of extraordinary success will emerge.

If you're like most of us, the past has been marked by challenges capturing that flow. Our performance, in the office, on the field, or on the court was merely a means to an end: the pursuit of winning no matter what the cost. Winning the next game. Making the next sale. Getting ahead. Somehow, in this fervent quest, we lost ourselves—or at least, the love of working and competing for the pure joy of the moment. We've been socialized to pursue the achievement-oriented path of promotions and victories at any expense, even with all the attachments of worry and concern and loss of integrity. The pats on the back we got gave us a feeling of validation, despite being accompanied by the self-consciousness and anxiety that came from trying to please others. In pursuing a better life, we lost the freedom to lead with the heart.

Our freedom got stymied by an endless stream of thoughts, most of which were negative or useless. We bounced back and forth from the past to the future, analyzing, pondering, hoping, doubting. It was like a never-ending seesaw, with the ground being the present moment, where extraordinary moments exist. We touched it and knew it was there, then quickly jumped to the past or future, joining our doubts and fears. Now, however, connected to our passion and purpose, we have the poise to counter the constant pressure and stress that used to flow through our heads and pull us away.

Life is vastly different. Ordinary moments become extraordinary. Excitement arises as we have more sacred moments—times where peace and passion come together, where effort becomes art. In the past, those moments were so unfamiliar and uncomfortable that we rushed back to pursue society-defined achievement and status. Sacred moments were unsettling because they imparted an awareness of our potential, and often we didn't want to face it. Perhaps we were afraid of what we might find and the fears we would have to confront. The possibility that we weren't living up to our potential, combined with the knowledge that the effort to do so may have required some degree of suffering and discomfort, was scary. Amazingly, we were more comfortable with the transient feelings of the seesaw than the grounded appreciation of what's possible: a life of extraordinary experiences and peak performance.

Now, times have changed. Today we begin to take more risks, to face our fears and fully experience sacred moments in both our careers and daily lives. We'll live with passion and courage, and we'll confront those times of fear and the desire for social acceptance with a determination to be our true selves and live each moment fully. Now we have a new mind-set, a new skill set, and new tool set. Everything has changed. We know that at any moment, we can transform our state, and live with more freedom, vision, and resonance.

Because of this, we commit to continue our search for truth in how to live, how to feel, and how to compete. We'll rise above our ever-changing circumstances and the wins and losses and get steadily more in tune with excellence, seeing the beauty and abundance around us, unconstrained by our emotions and perceived limitations.

Through this lens, our faith will continue to grow and sacred moments will unfold. Our perspective will continue to broaden, which will enable us, like a golfer standing over a ten-foot putt for the win, to have a steady hand, a clear mind, and an unburdened heart. It can be a scary path as you learn to be comfortable being uncomfortable and lose your attachment to the superficial. But the reward—connecting with your true self and the fullness of life that awaits—is worth it. It's always worth it.

Notes

Chapter 1

1   *Seduced by the siren*: Leonard, George. *Mastery*. New York: Plume, 1991.

4   *Maslow described eight elements*: Maslow, Abraham. *The Farther Reaches of Human Nature*. New York: Viking Press, 1971. For a summary of the eight behaviors go to abraham-maslow.com.

6   *According to Maslow*: Maslow, Abraham. *The Farther Reaches of Human Nature.*

7   *most people have a sickness*: Kierkegaard, Søren. *The Sickness unto Death*. New York: Penguin, 1989.

7   *I had expectations*: Marx, Jeffrey. *Season of Life*. New York: Simon and Schuster, 2003.

8   *The single biggest failure*: Marx, Jeffrey. *Season of Life.*

10   *TVI stifles your ability*: Christakis, Dimitri A., Frederick J. Zimmerman, et al. "Early Television Exposure and Subsequent Attentional Problems in Children." *Pediatrics* 113, no. 4 (April 2004).

10   *Television watching*: Doige, Norman, M.D. *The Brain That Changes Itself.* New York: Penguin, 2007.

10   *We're in a replay*: Trebelhorn, Tom. Private correspondence.

11   *Sport psychologist Dr. Keith Henschen says that*: Henschen, Keith, Ph.D. Private correspondence.

13   *In this win-at-all-costs society*: Dr. Bob Goldman surveyed 198 athletes asking them if they would take a drug guaranteeing victory in every competition but that it would kill them in five years. One hundred and three athletes said yes. Goldman, Bob. *Death in the Locker Room.* South Bend, IN: Icarus Press, 1984.

13   *To trade our soul*: The 440-horsepower 2009 Maserati GranTurismo S can do 0–100 km/h in 4.9 seconds, has a top speed of 295 km/h, and has a base price of $117,500. maserati.com.

14   *Our North Carolina players*: Smith, Dean. *The Carolina Way.* New York: Penguin, 2004.

14   *I haven't been happy*: Crouse, Karen. "Near Thirty, Swimmer Resumes Sport for the Young." *New York Times.* nytimes .com/2007/07/01/sports/othersports/01swim.html?ex= 1187409600&en=71951d6c796af0a0&ei=5070.

15   *We've become nothing*: Campbell, Joseph. *The Power of Myth.* New York: Doubleday, 1988.

16   *make our sense*: Loehr, Jim, Ph.D., and Peter McLaughlin. *Mental Toughness Training.* Niles, IL: Nightingale Conant, 1990. Audiocassette.

16   *Andrew B*: Andrew B. Private correspondence.

17   *a trip through Tibet*: Kehoe, John. *Mind Power into the Twenty-First Century.* Vancouver: Zoëtic, 1997.

18   *meet with Triumph*: Kipling, Rudyard. From the poem "If."
     kipling.org.uk/poems_if.htm.

18   *Success and failure*: Svetich, Ronn. Private correspondence.

19   *If we're constantly*: Krzyzewski, Mike. *Leading with the
     Heart*. New York: Warner Books, 2001.

20   *Jim Loehr says*: Loehr, Jim, Ph.D. *Mental Toughness Training
     for Sports*. Lexington, KY: Stephen Greene Press, 1986.

20   *For years I*: Botterill, Cal, Ph.D., and Tom Patrick, Ph.D.
     Perspective. Winnipeg: Lifeskills, 2003.

20   *Sport psychologist Jerry Lynch emphasizes*: Huang,
     Chungliang Al, and Jerry Lynch. *Thinking Body, Dancing
     Mind*. New York: Bantam Trade Paperback, 1994.

21   *Somehow top performers*: Botterill, Cal, Ph.D. Private
     correspondence.

Chapter 2

25   *We Western people*: Kelly, Thomas R. *A Testament of
     Devotion*. New York: Harper, 1941.

28   *In our everyday life*: Suzuki, Shunryu. *Zen Mind, Beginner's
     Mind*. New York: Weatherhill, 1970.

30   *the Trickster*: Kehoe, John. Private correspondence. John
     calls it the Great Trickster.

31   *This is not*: Wallace, David Foster. Kenyon College
     Commencement Address. May 21, 2005. http://online.wsj
     .com/article/SB122178211966454607.html.

33   *It's "hardwired into our boards at birth"*: Wallace, David
     Foster. Kenyon College Commencement Address.

36   *the mind becomes one*: Gallwey, Timothy. *The Inner Game of
     Tennis*. New York: Random House, 1974.

37 *recognize our ego defenses*: Maslow, Abraham. *The Farther Reaches of Human Nature.* New York: Viking Press, 1971.

38 *The biggest obstacle*: Botterill, Cal, Ph.D. Private correspondence.

38 *professor Caroline Dweck describes*: Dweck, Caroline. *Mindset.* New York: Ballantine Books, 2006.

39 *It's an absolute necessity*: Smith, Dean. *The Carolina Way.* New York: Penguin, 2004.

39 *nothing is "either good or bad"*: Shakespeare, William. *Hamlet.*

41 *Lance Armstrong, seven-time winner*: Armstrong, Lance. *It's Not About the Bike.* New York: Penguin, 2002.

42 *Perfectionism is*: Ravizza, Ken, Ph.D. Private correspondence.

43 *The D-slide begins*: Coppel, David, Ph.D. Private correspondence.

44 *These negative voices*: Nouwen, Henri. *Life of the Beloved.* New York: Crossroad Publishing, 1992.

45 *Primarily it's the athletes'*: Maher, Charlie, Ph.D. Private correspondence.

45 *Fusing with their language*: Maher, Charlie, Ph.D.

46 *With no exceptions*: Fannin, Jim. Private correspondence.

46 *As I'm sure*: Wallace, David Foster. Kenyon College Commencement Address. May 21, 2005.

Chapter 3

51 *On July 15*: Pugh, Lewis Gordon. Private correspondence.

52 *It doesn't think clearly*: Noakes, Tim. Private correspondence.

52 *Scientists around the world*: Pugh, Lewis Gordon, and Tim Noakes. Private correspondence.

54 *At best, I will*: Pugh, Lewis Gordon. Private correspondence.

54 *So, what pushes*: Pugh, Lewis Gordon.

55 *What animates [mountain] climbers*: O'Connell, Nicholas. *Beyond Risk*. Seattle: Mountaineers Books, 1995.

55 *I was in*: Pugh, Lewis Gordon. Private correspondence.

58 *Winning the gold medal*: Newburg, Doug, Ph.D. *The Most Important Lesson No One Ever Taught Me*. Bloomington, IN: Xlibris, 2006.

60 *It's what I did*: Streeter, Tanya. Private correspondence.

61 *Success, like happiness*: Frankl, Victor. *Man's Search for Meaning*. Boston: Beacon Press, 2006.

63 *To achieve peak*: Csikszentmihalyi, Mihaly, Ph.D. *Flow*. New York: Harper and Row, 1990.

63 *A grateful person*: Kubler-Ross, Elizabeth, and David Kessler. *Life Lessons*. New York: Scribner, 2000.

64 *Your team consists of*: Becker, David. Private correspondence.

65 *I'll tell you in a nutshell*: Maraniss, David. *When Pride Still Mattered: A Life of Vince Lombardi*. New York: Simon and Schuster, 1999.

Chapter 4

73 *A warrior considers*: Cleary, Thomas. *Code of the Samurai*. Boston: Tuttle, 1999.

74 *based largely on three values*: Nitobe, Inazo. *Bushido: The Soul of Japan*. Radford, VA: Wilder, 2008.

75   *This is the essence*: Yamamoto, Tsunetomo. *Bushido: The Way of the Warrior.* Garden City Park, New York: Square One, 2003.

76   *The most important trait*: Csikszentmihalyi, Mihaly, Ph.D. *Flow.* New York: Harper and Row, 1990.

77   *Mastering others*: Tzu, Lao. *Tao Te Ching.* New York: Harper Perennial, 2006.

79   *Your time is limited*: Jobs, Steve. Stanford University Commencement Address. June 14, 2005. http://news-service .stanford.edu/news/2005/june15/jobs-061505.html.

81   *The greatest most single*: Orlick, Terry, and Shauna Burke. "Mental Strategies of Elite Mount Everest Climbers." *Journal of Excellence,* Issue No. 8, 2003.

82   *Dostoevsky said*: Frankl, Victor. *Man's Search for Meaning.* Boston: Beacon Press, 2006.

84   *The 12-step model*: Alcoholics Anonymous. Go to aa.org for a description of the 12 steps.

85   *The illness in all*: Kurtz, Ernest. *Not-God: A History of Alcoholics Anonymous.* Center City, PA: Hazelden, 1991.

85   *New York Giants football*: Lapointe, Joe. "Hoping to Return, Tyree Keeps Faith." *New York Times.* October 12, 2008. nytimes.com/2008/10/13/sports/football/13giants.html.

87   *Team captain Sean Hurley*: Hurley, Sean. Private correspondence.

89   *Vocation comes from*: Buechner, Frederick. *Wishful Thinking: A Seeker's ABC.* San Francisco: Harper, 1993.

Chapter 5

93   *Most people who have*: Deutschman, Alan. *Change or Die.* New York: HarperCollins, 2007.

94   *We don't have power*: Kehoe, John. *Mind Power into the Twenty-First Century.* Vancouver: Zoëtic, 1997.

95   *seven basic emotions*: Botterill, Cal, Ph.D., and Tom Patrick, Ph.D. *Perspective.* Winnipeg: Lifeskills, 2003.

96   *What gets your*: Johnson, Darrell. From the sermon "Therefore, do not worry." Tenth Avenue Alliance, Vancouver, BC, January 11, 2009.

97   *The proper emotional response*: Loehr, Jim, Ph.D. *Mental Toughness Training for Sports.* Lexington, KY: Stephen Greene Press, 1986.

98   *Those dominated by*: Willard, Dallas, Ph.D. *Renovation of the Heart.* Colorado Springs: VanPress, 2002.

100   *Video games seem*: Chan, Philip A., and Terry Rabinowitz. "A Cross-Sectional Analysis of Video Games and Attention Deficit Hyperactivity Disorder Symptoms in Adolescents." *Annals of General Psychiatry* 5, no.16 (2006).

102   *In his book*: Maisel, Eric, Ph.D. *Coaching the Artist Within.* Novato, CA: New World Library, 2005.

104   *Erica K.*: Erica K. Private correspondence.

107   *Try this exercise*: This is a common visualization; you can find a similar one in *NLP: The New Technology of Achievement.* Andreas, Steve, and Charles Faulkner. New York: William Morrow, 1994.

108   *Here is a powerful exercise*: Bandler, Richard, and John Grinder. *Frogs into Princes: Neuro Linguistic Programming.* Boulder, CO: Real People Press, 1979.

Chapter 6

113   *Tyrone ran for the fence*: Bogues, Tyrone, and David Levine. *In the Land of Giants.* Boston: Little, Brown, 1994.

113 *It wasn't an easy life*: Bogues, Tyrone, and David Levine. *In the Land of Giants.*

119 *We delete, distort, and generalize*: Bandler, Richard, and John Grinder. *The Structure of Magic*. Palo Alto: Science and Behavior Books, 1975.

120 *To the outside world*: Bogues, Tyrone, and David Levine. *In the Land of Giants.*

125 *You are only*: Fannin, Jim. *S.C.O.R.E. for Life*. New York: William Morrow, 2006.

125 *I hit solid*: Fannin, Jim. Private correspondence.

125 *Decathlete gold medalist Bruce Jenner*: Novelguide.com. novelguide.com/a/discover/nspf_02/nspf_02_00271.html.

127 *Callista said that*: Callista B. Private correspondence.

131 *Alan Deutschman's book*: Deutschman, Alan. *Change or Die*. New York: HarperCollins, 2007.

Chapter 7

135 *The true worth of a man:* Aurelius, Marcus. famousquotesandauthors.com.

137 *It's like playing golf*: Andrew R. Private correspondence.

140 *The ultimate goal*: Funakoshi, Gichin. *Karate-Do Kyohan*. New York: Kodansha International, 1973.

140 *Your heart has room*: Bonhoeffer, Dietrich. *The Cost of Discipleship*. New York: Touchstone, 1995.

141 *Abraham Maslow described*: Maslow, Abraham. *The Farther Reaches of Human Nature*. New York: Viking Press, 1971.

141 *I create a simple mind*: Svetich, Ronn. Private correspondence.

145 *Dr. Viktor Frankl puts it*: Frankl, Viktor. *Man's Search for Meaning*. Boston: Beacon Press, 2006.

146   *Try to discover beauty*: Stanislavsky, Konstantin. *An Actor Prepares*. New York: Theater Arts, 1989.

148   *All of our invented fears*: Kubler-Ross, Elizabeth, and David Kessler. *Life Lessons*. New York: Scribner, 2000.

149   *I never prayed*: Parent, Joseph, Ph.D. *Zen Golf*. New York: Doubleday, 2002.

152   *I think a lack*: Abrams, Jonathan. "Louisville Has Too Much of Everything for Arizona." *New York Times*. nytimes.com/2009/03/28/sports/ncaabasketball/28louisville.html?_r=1&scp=1&sq=louisville%20basketball%20arizona&st=cse.

153   *If your most talented*: Tressel, Jim, Chris Fabry, and John Maxwell. *The Winner's Manual*. Carol Stream, IL: Tyndale House, 2008.

153   *Definitely. Humility can*: Joe D. Private correspondence.

154   *Mimi Silbert, CEO*: delanceystreetfoundation.org.

154   *Busyness is the most*: Merton, Thomas. *New Seeds of Contemplation*. New York: New Directions, 1972.

155   *If you don't take time*: Covey, Stephen R. *The Seven Habits of Highly Successful People*. New York: Simon and Schuster, 1989.

Chapter 8

159   *The mind should be*: Musashi, Miyamoto and Thomas Cleary. *The Book of Five Rings*. Boston: Shambhala, 2005.

159   *Brace for impact*: CBS. "Flight 1549: A Routine Takeoff Turns Ugly." February 8, 2009. cbsnews.com/stories/2009/02/08/60minutes/main4783580_page3.shtml.

163   *If you're a hockey player*: Brown, Matt. Private correspondence.

164   *Her medals are*: Botterill, Cal, Ph.D., and Tom Patrick, Ph.D. *Perspective*. Winnipeg: Lifeskills, 2003.

165   *Their perspective about*: Bauman, Jim, Ph.D. Private correspondence.

167   *Even as we're being*: Jackson, Phil, and Hugh Delehanty. *Sacred Hoops*. New York: Hyperion, 1995.

167   *In one notable moment*: Saporito, Bill. "Rebel on the Edge." *Time*. January 23, 2006.

168   *The opponent is not*: Jackson, Phil, and Hugh Delehanty. *Sacred Hoops*.

168   *Keeping the want to*: Botterill, Cal, Ph.D. Private correspondence.

170   *His research resulted*: Newburg, Doug, Ph.D. *The Most Important Lesson No One Ever Taught Me*. Bloomington, IN: Xlibris, 2006.

171   *he never managed*: Trebelhorn, Tom. Private correspondence.

171   *If I was*: Towers, Kevin. Private correspondence.

172   *My initial reaction*: CBS. "Flight 1549."

173   *I think, in many ways*: CBS. "Flight 1549."

174   *The resident performed*: Tribble, Curt, M.D., and Doug Newburg, Ph.D. "Learning to Fly: Teaching Mental Strategies to Future Surgeons." *Journal of Excellence*. Issue No. 1, 1998. zoneofexcellence.ca/journal/issue01/learning _to_fly.pdf.

175   *The moment you dive*: Tutton, Mark. "Lewis Pugh: The Human Polar Bear." http://edition.cnn.com/2009/health/ 02/25/lewis.pugh/index.html.

Chapter 9

181   *He's not going to*: Private correspondance with Ken Ravizza, Ph.D., who told me what Lou said.

181   *When asked why*: Karelin, Alexander. wikipedia.com.

182   *After the Olympics*: Crouse, Karen. "Crocker Enjoying His Ride to Beijing." New York Times. nytimes.com/2008/ 08/04/sports/olympics/04swimmer.html?scp=6&sq=ian %20crocker&st=cse.

182   *Silbert's fundamentals of success*: delanceystreetfoundation .org.

189   *When you argue*: Brown, Les. *Live Your Dreams*. New York: HarperCollins, 1994.

190   *We must embrace failure*: Bertman, Skip. Private correspondence.

191   *In our scriptures*: Suzuki, Shunryu. *Zen Mind, Beginner's Mind*. New York: Weatherhill, 1970.

193   *Our preoccupation with goals*: Leonard, George. *Mastery*. New York: Plume, 1991.

195   *Louisiana State University swimmer*: Colleen B. Private correspondence.

198   *Even more challenging*: Kubler-Ross, Elizabeth, and David Kessler. *Life Lessons*. New York: Scribner, 2000.

Chapter 10

203   *Jim Tressel, head football coach*: Crouse, Karen. "Coach Keeps Truths and Swim Titles Flowing," *New York Times*. http://www.nytimes.com/2009/02/25/sports/othersports/ 25swim.html?_r=1

204   *Jackson instilled*: Jackson, Phil, and Hugh Delehanty. *Sacred Hoops*. New York: Hyperion, 1995.

204   *It has always been*: Vermeil, Dick. Speech given at Bellevue Community College, Bellevue, Washington. Circa 1987.

205   *He defined success*: Wooden, John. *Wooden on Leadership*. New York: McGraw-Hill, 2005.

205   *Jim Tressel slightly*: Tressel, Jim, Chris Fabry, and John Maxwell. *The Winner's Manual*. Carol Stream, IL: Tyndale House, 2008.

206   *[Tressel] builds his program*: Mandel, Stewart. "Best Around? These Three Qualities Have Made Tressel Great Coach." *Sports Illustrated*. http://sportsillustrated.cnn.com/2007/ writers/stewart_mandel/01/07/tressel.

206   *According to* Sports Illustrated: Guterson, David. "Frosty the Showman." *Sports Illustrated*. http://vault.sportsillustrated .cnn.com/vault/article/magazine/MAG1005843/index.htm

206   *Before a big game*: Westering, Frosty. Private correspondence.

206   *John Wooden didn't scout*: Wooden, John. *Wooden on Leadership*. New York: McGraw-Hill, 2005.

207   *The only way to beat*: Kim, W. Chan, and Renee Mauborgne. *Blue Ocean Strategy*. Boston: Harvard Business School Press, 2005.

207   *The most successful companies*: Collins, Jim. *Built to Last*. New York: HarperCollins, 1997.

208   *Defining best*: Westering, Frosty. Private correspondence.

210   *With the Bulls*: Jackson, Phil, and Hugh Delehanty. *Sacred Hoops*.

210   *In* The Power of Story: Loehr, Jim, Ph.D. *The Power of Story*. New York: Free Press, 2007.

210   *Find a place within yourself*: Crouse, Karen. "Coach Keeps Truths and Swim Titles Flowing," *New York Times*.

211   *Jim Collins's research*: Collins, Jim. *Built to Last.*

211   *Goals are important*: Tressel, Jim, Chris Fabry, and John
       Maxwell. *The Winner's Manual.*

213   *I focused on*: Jeff N. Private correspondence.

214   *According to one study*: Albert Mehrabian conducted studies
       on communication and the impact of nonverbal messages
       that have come to be known as the 7%-38%-55% Rule.
       http://en.wikipedia.org/wiki/albert_mehrabian.

215   *The pursuit of a single goal*: Crouse, Karen. "Coach Keeps
       Truths and Swim Titles Flowing," *New York Times.*

217   *In 2002, before*: Drape, Joe. "College Football: This Time,
       Coker and Tressel Meet on the Field." *New York Times.*
       nytimes.com/2003/01/03/sports/college-football
       -this-time-coker-and-tressel-meet-on-the-field.html.

217   *Phil Jackson cites*: Jackson, Phil, and Hugh Delehanty.
       Sacred Hoops.

Glossary

abundance mind-set: The mind-set of seeing possibilities, opportunities, and richness of life. An abundance mind-set comes from always looking for the positive, tuning into beauty, and being grateful.

affirmation: A positive statement about who or how you want to be or what you want to achieve in the future, as if it were true today. For example: I am an incredible public speaker. I live in a world of abundance. I am poised under pressure.

affluenza: The insecurity that arises from placing your identity in money, possessions, achievements, or status. This "virus" causes an endless desire for more of any of those four elements because it never truly satisfies. Many people carry the virus unknowingly until their deaths.

best self: The person within that emerges when you rid yourself of all that's not you; you when you're most powerful; a synonym for the true self.

Note: *These are the working definitions for this book, which may differ from your dictionary.*

centering (getting centered): The process of bringing your energy to the center of your body, just below the belly button; clearing the mind through deep breathing and focused concentration.

conscious mind: The part of the mind's workings of which you are aware and that does the thinking.

courage: The ability to be fully present at what matters most.

Critic: The part of the mind that judges everything and labels it good or bad, to which you then react emotionally. The Critic is attached to your circumstances.

dreams: The intense feelings that come when you're fully present doing what you love. Goals are set in order to feel the dream.

ego: The part of the mind most susceptible to the affluenza virus, finding identity through money, possessions, achievements, and/or status. It is the great barrier because it is never satisfied and is constantly under threat.

emotions: A subset of feelings; there are seven basic emotions: happiness, interest, surprise, fear, anger, guilt, and sadness.

feelings: The state or condition of your mental, physical, and emotional self. Feelings include emotions, sensations, and desires.

fixed mind-set: The mind-set that personal talents, skills, and abilities are mostly genetic. For example: your IQ cannot be improved. To a person with a fixed mind-set, a failure comes from a lack of talent or skill.

fully present: A moment of peace, focus, and clarity; a heightened awareness, with no needs, concerns, or thoughts of the past or the future.

goals: External objectives set in order to live your dreams. There are outcome goals (not in your full control) and process goals (focused on the process of achieving an outcome; much more in your control).

growth mind-set: The mind-set that personal talents, skills, and abilities are mostly determined by effort, perseverance, and learning.

homeostasis: The efforts of the subconscious mind to maintain a certain level of skill or achievement, that which you believe is right for you. For example, if you are performing above what you believe you are capable of doing, your subconscious will try to bring the performance down to your comfort level; it also works in the other direction when you're underperforming.

love: The ability to lead with the heart; an intense feeling focused on something outside of the self: other people, a performance, making a difference, and so forth. The word is mostly used herein to describe intense passion for life and for the moment. Love (outward focused) overcomes fear (inward focused).

mind-set: A habitual state of mind.

Monkey Mind: The endless flow of thoughts, mostly negative and/or unproductive.

monster of self: The self-centered human nature that, undisciplined, moves toward fear.

purpose beyond yourself: A purpose that directs your life and gives it meaning. With a strong enough purpose, people will give their lives in exchange for it.

reboot: To turn off the mind and turn it back on. Doing so stops the Monkey Mind; part of getting centered.

resonance: The feeling of being fully present doing what you love. Usually has the best chance of occurring when your gifts are challenged in a meaningful way.

scarcity mind-set: A negative mind-set that sees problems first and gets weighed down by unconstructive thoughts.

self-acceptance: Peace of mind that comes from realizing your unique value regardless of money, possessions, achievements, or status.

self-actualization: The journey toward Zoë; a life experienced fully, vividly, and selflessly, with full concentration and total absorption; the feeling of long-term fulfillment, accompanied by a purpose beyond the self; the peace and fulfillment present when life has meaning.

self-awareness: Consciousness of your thoughts, feelings, and actions and the ability to see them objectively, in order to grow. The ability to see your own patterns of thinking, feeling, and behavior and how they affect your life and those around you. Self-awareness is the first step toward growth and Zoë.

self-care: Controlling your energy in order to be your best self. Eating healthily, exercising regularly, thinking positively, visualizing, and getting centered are all examples of self-care.

self-centeredness: Attachment to your past; preoccupation with self; the natural limited viewpoint that fuels self-consciousness and the ego; with constant self-focus, your limits and failures continually emerge.

self-concern: The focus on self that leads to doubt, anxiety, and eventually fear.

self-conscious: Uncomfortably conscious of yourself; the feeling of discomfort from being noticed and perhaps judged by others.

selflessness: Putting the greater good in front of individual desires or needs. Selflessness helps everyone, including the selfless individual.

self-mastery: The self-control and presence that come when your life is focused on love, wisdom, and courage; pursuit of self-awareness, self-discipline, and self-education in order to grow to be your best self. The journey toward Zoë, which supersedes external achievements or worldly success.

self-rejection: Personalization of failure. Rather than objectively analyzing a setback or an unwanted outcome, you feel as if you not only failed in the task but also are a failure as a person, or you feel like less of a person because of some external event.

self-talk: The internal dialogue that goes on in the conscious mind.

sense of self: Your feeling of value; your sense of identity. If you have a strong sense of self, you are comfortable being uncomfortable, need no validation, are comfortable in your own skin, and do not rely strictly on successful outcomes to feel good as a person. A person with a weak sense of self lives in constant comparison with others and continually looks to satisfy the needs of the ego.

state: The condition of your mental, physical, and emotional self; feelings.

subconscious mind: The part of the mind that works beyond your awareness, allowing you to function and not think of every little thing (such as tying your shoes, walking, and breathing). The subconscious mind is continually being programmed to make your habitual thoughts and beliefs reality.

Trickster: The voice that reminds you of all your failures and projects them as future probabilities; the part of the mind that tells you why you cannot improve, win this match, or achieve your goals.

true self: The best part of you that emerges when you rid yourself of all that's not you; the part of you unattached to worldly success; your best self.

wisdom: Keen insight on how to live; the expanded vision that sees unobstructed views of beauty, opportunities, and connections with others.

Zoë: Absolute fullness of life; the state of being possessed of vitality; life, real and genuine; vigor and vibrancy of life; the culmination of love, wisdom, and courage; self-actualization.

Index

Absorption, total, 4
Accept this moment, 147–51
Affirmations, 127–30, 134
Affluenza virus
    description of, 6–10, 221
    fuel for, 10–12
Alcoholics Anonymous (AA), 85
Alfieri, Conte Vittorio, xvii
Anchoring and releasing different
    states, 105–9
Anxiety, 31–32, 43
Aristotle, 93
Armstrong, Lance, 41
Attachments, eight, 86–90
Attention, where to place your,
    96–97
Aurelius, Marcus, 135

Bandler, Richard, 108
Bauman, Jim, 165
Beauty, tuning into, 135–36, 144–47
Becker, David, 64

Beliefs
    changing, 126–27
    defined, 94, 133
    goals and, 130–31
    nature of, 115–17
Bertman, Skip, 190
Best, defining, 208–9
Blair, Bonnie, 165
Blue Ocean Strategy, 207
Bogues, Tyrone Muggsy, 113–14,
    120, 132
Bonhoeffer, Dietrich, 140
Boredom, 130
Botterill, Cal, 20, 21, 38, 66, 168
Brain That Changes Itself, The, 10
Breathing, deep, 101–2
Brown, Les, 189
Brown, Matt, 163
Buechner, Frederick, 89
Built to Last, 207
Burke, Shauna, 81
Busyness, 154–55, 156

Campbell, Joseph, 15
Centering exercises, 101–5
Chopra, Deepak, 147
Churchill, Winston, 81, 129
Clear perspective, 163–65
Coaching the Artist Within, 102
Coker, Larry, 217
Collins, Jim, 207, 211
Compliments, 152
Confidence, 164
Coppel, David, 43
Courage, 66–67, 68
Covey, Stephen, 155
Critic, the, 30, 31, 32, 39–41, 54, 173
Crocker, Ian, 182, 199
Csikszentmihalyi, Mihaly, 63, 76
Currie, Dan, 65

Death, 55, 73, 80
Delancey Street Foundation, 131–32, 182
Desire, power of, 97–99, 139
Deutschman, Alan, 93, 131
Discipline
    defined, 15–16
    positive energy and, 59, 60, 68, 69, 138
Doige, Norman, 10
Dostoevsky, Fyodor, 82
Doubts, 34
Dreams versus goals, 58–59
D-slide, 43
Dweck, Caroline, 38

Ego
    mastery versus, 78
    outcome and, 37–39
    on path to fear, 32
Ego defenses, lack of, 5
Ehrmann, Joe, 7–9

Eight attachments, 86–90
Einstein, Albert, 123
Emerson, Ralph Waldo, 153, 221
Emotional preparation, 172–74
Enjoyment and positive energy, 59, 68, 69, 138
Enron, 13
Entitlement, 151
Exercise, 100
Expectations, 102–4
Experience, structure of, 117–20

Failure, 18, 39, 125, 190–92
Fannin, Jim, 46, 125
Fear
    path to, 32
    root cause of, 27–30
Fearlessness, road to, 54–56
Feelings
    desires and, 97–99
    memories and, 109–10
    seven basic emotions, 95
    thoughts and, 96
Fiennes, Sir Ranulph, 52
Filter, adjusting your, 120–26
Five-second rule, 125
Focus
    positive energy and, 59, 60, 68, 69, 138
    simple mind, 140–44
Frankl, Viktor, 61, 82, 145
Franklin, Benjamin, 135
Full engagement
    accept this moment, 147–51
    be aware of your humanity, 151–55
    courage and, 66–67
    elements of being fully present, 138
    four ways to be fully present, 137, 156

power of, 137–40
simple mind, 140–44
tuning into beauty, 144–47

Gallwey, Timothy, 36
Gandhi, Mahatma, 81, 96
Generalization, 122
Goals
  beliefs and, 130–31
  dreams versus, 58–59
  purpose and, 211
  reminders of, 124
Good to Great, 207
Gratitude, 63, 152–53
Grinder, John, 108
Growth choices, 4
Growth concepts
  challenge what you know,
    186–89
  don't take things personally,
    196–98
  fail valiantly, 190–92
  five core concepts, 183
  key points about, 199–201
  master in-between moments,
    192–96
  sense of self, 184–86
Growth over fear, 198–99

Hemingway, Ernest, 141
Henschen, Keith, 11
High quality of life (HQL), 11
Holtz, Lou, 203
Honesty, 4
Hornung, Paul, 65
Hughes, Clara, 20, 164
Humanity, being aware of your,
  151–55
Humility, 152–54
Hurley, Sean, 87

In-between moments, 192–96
Innakoshi, Gichin, 140
Internet and television, 10–11, 26, 100
Intuition, 4

Jackson, Phil, 167, 168, 203, 204, 207,
  210, 217
Jenkins, Malcolm, 206
Jenner, Bruce, 125–26
Jobs, Steve, 79
Jones, E. Stanley, 96
Jordan, Michael, 39, 40, 190, 204,
  217–18
Journals
  for collecting thoughts, 156–57,
    172
  for recording attachments, 91
  for self-awareness, 155

Karelin, Alexander, 181, 199
Kehoe, John, 17, 94
Kelly, Thomas R., 25
Kierkegaard, Søren, 7
Kim, W. Chan, 207
King, Martin Luther, 81, 178
Kipling, Rudyard, 18
Kramer, Jerry, 65
Krzyzewski, Mike, 19, 178
Kubler-Ross, Elizabeth, 63, 148, 198

Lau-tzu, 77
Leaders, habits of
  connect individuals with vision
    beyond themselves, 212–15
  redefine success, 205–12
  seek self-mastery, 216–19
  three, 204–5
Leadership
  defined, 204
  key points about, 219–20

Lee, Bruce, 139
Leonard, George, 1, 193
Life Diamond, 67–70
Loehr, Jim, 16, 20, 97, 210, 211
Lombardi, Vince, 65
Love, 59–62, 67, 68, 70
Lynch, Jerry, 20

Madoff, Bernie, 13
Maher, Charlie, 45, 46
Maisel, Eric, 102
Mandala, the, 17
Mandela, Nelson, 81, 82, 178
Marconi, Guglielmo, 135
Marx, Jeffrey, 7
Masculinity, 8
Maslow, Abraham, 3, 4, 5, 6, 12, 37, 56, 63, 141, 216
Mastery
  defined, 57
  detours off path of, 62
  ego versus, 78
  foundation for, 69
  spirit of, 75–77
Mastery orientation, 166–67
Mauborgne, Renee, 207
Memories versus current feelings, 109–10
Mencken, H. L., 51
Merton, Thomas, 154
Michelangelo, 5, 137
Miller, Bode, 167
Mind Power into the Twenty-First Century, 17
Mind-set for growth
  challenge what you know, 186–89
  don't take things personally, 196–98
  fail valiantly, 190–92

five core concepts, 183
key points about, 199–201
master in-between moments, 192–96
sense of self, 184–86
Monkey Mind, 30, 31, 32, 44–46, 54, 142, 144, 173
Most Important Lesson No One Ever Taught Me, The, 58
Mother Teresa, 81
Multitasking, 142
Musashi, Miyamoto, 159

Navy Seals, 212–13
Negative thoughts
  counteracting, 124–25
  detaching from, 143–44
Newburg, Doug, 58, 170
Noakes, Tim, 51, 52, 175
Nouwen, Henri, 44
Nutrition, 100

Obama, Barack, 129
Obsession with outcome, 37–39
Obsession with self, 33–34
Obsession with winning, 12–17
O'Connell, Nicholas, 55
Orlick, Terry, 81
Osborne, Tom, 14
Osterman, Cat, 126, 127
Overanalysis, 11, 38, 44–46

Pavlov, Ivan, 106
Peak experiences, 5, 21
Perfectionism, 42
Perspective, 20, 21
Perspective, clear, 163–65
Physiology, controlling, 99–102
Piniella, Lou, 181
Pitino, Rick, 152

Poise
  clear perspective, 163–65
  connection with performance,
      168–78
  essence of, 161–63
  four keys to, 163
  key points about, 179
  in Life Diamond, 68, 69
  mastery orientation, 166–67
  positive rivalry, 167–68
Present, being fully. *See* Full
  engagement
Process of success, 17–20
Pugh, Lewis Gordon, xviii, 51, 52,
      53, 54–56, 64, 65, 66, 67, 86,
      126, 175, 212

Quinlan, Bill, 65

Rapport, building, 214–15
Ravizza, Ken, 42
Relaxation
  importance of, 101–2
  positive energy and, 59, 60, 68,
      69, 138
Resonance, 68, 69, 141, 161, 169,
      223
Reverence, 216
Rivalry, positive, 167–68
Rodriguez, Alex, 125
Rodriguez, Chi Chi, 149

Sacred moments, 2, 21
Samurai, paradox of the, 74–75
Season of Life, 7
Self, strong sense of, 61–62,
      184–86
Self-acceptance, 3, 62, 185
Self-actualization, 3–5, 46, 56,
      216

Self-awareness, 4, 34–36
Self-centeredness
  fear and, 27–30
  inner battle with, 31–33
  obsession with self, 33–34
  self-awareness versus, 34–36
Self-consciousness, 29, 32, 152,
      197
Self-development, 4–5
Self-doubt, 34
Self-mastery, spirit of, 57, 62, 69,
      75–77, 78
Self-rejection, 42, 43, 44
Service to others, 85–86
Shakespeare, William, 39
Shigesuke, Taira, 73
Siddhartha, Gautama, 113
Silbert, Mimi, 132, 154, 182, 199
Simple mind, 140–44
Smith, Bob, 85
Smith, Dean, 14, 39
Staley, Dawn, 58, 164, 212
Stanislavsky, Konstantin, 146
Starr, Bart, 65
Steen, Jim, 203, 204, 210, 215
Streeter, Tanya, 60–61
Success
  process of, 17–20
  redefining, 205–12
Suffering, 80–84
Sullenberger, Chesley, 159–60, 172,
      173, 174
Suzuki, Shunryu, 28, 191
Svetich, Ronn, 18, 141
Swagger, 59, 60, 68, 69, 100, 138,
      171–72

Tao of Leadership, The, 217
Television and Internet (TVI), 10–11,
      26, 100

Thoreau, Henry David, 13, 44
Thoughts. *See also* Monkey Mind
  attachment to, 47–48
  counteracting negative, 124–25
  detaching from negative, 143–44
Time-outs, 155, 157
Towers, Kevin, 171
Trebelhorn, Tom, 10, 171
Tressel, Jim, 153, 203, 204, 205,
  206, 211, 217
Tribble, Curt, 173, 174
Trickster, the, 30, 31, 32, 41–44,
  54, 125, 173
True self, 59, 61–62
Tunnell, Emlen, 65
12-step model, 84–86
Tyree, David, 85

Vallerand, Robert, 95
Vermeil, Dick, 204
Visualization, 174–78, 180

Walking with a swagger, 59,
  60, 68, 69, 100, 138,
  171–72
Wallace, David Foster, 31, 33,
  46
Westering, Frosty, 206, 208
Willard, Dallas, 98
Wilson, Bill, 85
Winning, obsession with,
  12–17
Wisdom, 62–66, 67, 68
Wooden, John, 178, 205, 206–7
Woods, Tiger, 139, 167

Yamamoto, Tsunetomo, 75

Zen Mind, Beginner's Mind,
  191
Zoë, 56–57, 59, 60, 67–70, 74,
  84, 136, 151, 181, 183, 185,
  186, 192, 223